The Development of the Language Arts

THE PROFESSIONAL EDUCATION SERIES

Walter K. Beggs, *Editor*
Dean Emeritus
Teachers College
University of Nebraska

Royce H. Knapp, *Research Editor*
Regents Professor of Education
Teachers College
University of Nebraska

The Development of the Language Arts

From Birth Through Elementary School

86758

by

GORDON GREENE

Associate Professor of Elementary Education
University of Nebraska

PROFESSIONAL EDUCATORS PUBLICATIONS, INC.
LINCOLN, NEBRASKA

For Our Children
Kelli, Todd, and Ben

Library of Congress Catalog Card No.: 73-85548

ISBN   0-88224-050-1

Contents

PREFACE 7

1. LANGUAGE DEVELOPMENT AFTER BIRTH 8

Language Development During Infancy 8
Vocabulary Development 9
The Development of Grammatical Structure 10
Factors That Influence Language Development 11
Generalizations About Language Development 12

2. LANGUAGE DEVELOPMENT IN PRESCHOOL PROGRAMS . . . 14

Experience with Language 14
The Teacher—A Facilitator 15
The Development of Listening 16
The Role of Literature 18
Reading to Children 20
Oral Communication 22
Preschool Reading 24
Preschool Handwriting 26

3. LANGUAGE ARTS PROGRAM IN THE ELEMENTARY SCHOOL . . 29

Oral Expression 30
Written Expression 41
Spelling 53
Foreign Language in the Elementary School 56
Reading 57
Evaluation in the Language Arts 64

NOTES 74

INDEX 78

CHAPTER 1

Language Development After Birth

A child's language development begins the moment he hears language — usually with the informal language activities of the home. Although the quality of this language will vary greatly from one home to another, learning is certain to take place. Increasingly, as early childhood education has been rediscovered, early language learning has become a concern of educators and parents. Sociologists have rediscovered the fact that social class affects language learning, psychologists have rediscovered the work of Jean Piaget, and many are reminded that economic conditions produce an environment that affects the life-style of a child in many ways — including the development of his language.

LANGUAGE DEVELOPMENT DURING INFANCY

The child begins to learn from the world around him from the very moment of birth. The first few weeks of life are spent in a rather passive role, with the child the recipient of attention from adults who are significant in his life. As a basic means for bringing about change the child utilizes vocalization, although movement of limbs may also have some effect. His early vocalizations appear to have no fixed pattern of meaning: crying can indicate relief from either hunger or pain. By the third or fourth month of life, the child's babbling is influenced by the language he hears and he begins to "practice." With this practice comes evidence of control of volume, pitch, and articulation, as shown by his ability to repeat these features.

The child's ability to communicate increases steadily. His eyes glisten, his shoulders tense, his breathing quickens, and he smiles when he is lifted by the mother. He coos, he giggles, he may even smile back, responding to continuous reinforcement by the alert mother.

Before long the child is able to amuse himself for longer periods of time. He may coo and babble to himself as he bangs objects on the tray of his high chair or as he shifts a finger toy from one hand to the other. He begins to listen more intently to words spoken by others and learns to recognize differences in volume between the voices of his mother and his father. He may be delighted with the noise made by a certain toy and will repeat it many times. Frustration with his inability to move a certain object may bring forth a rage of crying or intent jabbering.

His ability to respond to a social world continually increases. At around forty weeks he may be able to wave bye-bye and attempt to pat-a-cake. Not only does he respond to gestures, facial expressions, and sounds but he may heed *no-no*. He enjoys the give-and-take of social games such as "peek-a-boo," and giggles with pleasure in a game of "chase-as-he-creeps."

It is at these times that opportunities for increasing the child's linguistic abilities are paramount. Opportunity for use of these communicative forms, independently and in combination, is an indispensable prerequisite to later, more articulate use of language. The wise parent, regardless of the economic standards in the home, will consistently spend time with the child in the give-and-take of social interaction. Individual differences in the rate and quality of language development may be evidenced during this period.

The child's first "words" may not be words as adults know them. He may say *da-da* as a result of experimentation with the vocal apparatus. Of course, to the parents this is his first word and, especially if he is the first child, an entry will be made in the baby-book of the exact date and time of the event.

The child is merely naming things—anyone who comes into the room could be what *da-da* means. It is some time later, when verbal sounds are closely associated with objects, people, or activities, that the first true words are spoken. From this point on language is commonly used as an indication of mental development. These first "words" are particularly important to the child. They are basic in the development of his phonological (sound) system. As the child says these first "words," he is beginning the acquisition of phonemes (the smallest units of meaningful speech sound).

VOCABULARY DEVELOPMENT

In some instances, intentional words may not have a communicative function but are produced on cue. The parents urge the child to say *bye-bye* until he does. The response of the parents when he succeeds in saying the word is highly gratifying to him, and future desires for similar gratification may cause the child to utter *bye-bye* every time he sees someone with a coat.

The child has developed a unit of language. When he is in a situation that is related to a felt need, such as satisfaction of hunger, he may say *eat*. This one word is associated with the total situation. Although limited in the number of phonemes, these words are giant steps toward gaining the sounds of adult speech.

At the same time the child is developing the ability to generalize, to find some pattern in the situations he experiences. He may notice that *no* occurs in many situations that have a negative aspect. Thus, he may experiment with using *no* in many of his attempts in similar situations.

The present discussion of the development of vocabulary in children could be misleading. Gifted children may be more advanced in speech development whereas retarded children would be much slower. Many children, regardless of intelligence, are slow in vocabulary development because they have received little reinforcement or because their needs have been met without their having to speak.

THE DEVELOPMENT OF GRAMMATICAL STRUCTURE

Up to this point the child's speech has closely resembled the speech models of the parents or adults. As the child becomes aware of a need for language usage, attempting to construct utterances according to his own rules, his language may be viewed as ungrammatical by adult standards. He may say, "I tooked it," because he is aware of some general rule for forming the past tense. Parents should not be disturbed about such errors in the child's speech. It is too early for the child to have control over all the rules — he is in the process of sorting them out. The point is that the child must not be criticized for making errors at this stage. Criticism for experimentation with generalizations may cause him to be reluctant to make future attempts and he could remain passive in this aspect of language development.

Weir reported that her young son, while lying in the crib, engaged in linguistic play that revealed his pulling utterances with similar patterns out of his experience, which he then experimented with.[1] Chomsky believes that grammatical speech is a built-in human inclination.[2] Ervin and Miller conclude that by age four most children have learned the fundamental structural features of their language.[3]

The extent to which a young child experiments with his language until he gets it organized into a system, and the fact that not all his speech is imitation, appears to substantiate the above results. Piaget points out that when children are presented with an idea to be learned in adult language, structures are being forced on their thinking, and he asks whether it is proper to teach the structure or to present the child with situations where he is active and creates the structure himself. He believes that when we teach too fast, we keep the child from inventing and discovering for himself.[4]

FACTORS THAT INFLUENCE LANGUAGE DEVELOPMENT

At this time it is not clear whether the child gains language power as a result of high intelligence or gains high intelligence as a result of language power.[5] Studies reveal that relationships exist between intelligence and various measures of language — such as, positive correlations between measures of intelligence and the amount of vocabulary, ability to articulate, and language maturity.[6]

Jensen believes that intelligence is determined largely by heredity and cannot be altered significantly by improving environment.[7] Although there is much disagreement among the arguments advanced against his study, they do seem to support the beliefs that we are not in a position to say with certainty whether there are genetic racial differences in intelligence, and that we cannot ascertain the degree of impact upon intelligence that is possible through environmental changes.

Since most tests of intelligence are dependent upon the use of language, it is difficult to determine what the relationships between measures of language and of intelligence mean. There is, however, reason to believe that the level at which language functions is one of the most important indicators of the level of higher thought.

The child's physical equipment also has an influence upon language acquisition and development. The speech organs (teeth, tongue, lips, throat), the organs of hearing, and the neuromuscular system all must work effectively in order for a child's language development to reveal normal progress. Vision handicaps can also interfere with language development.

Sex differences have been considered influential factors in the development of language. Earlier studies pointed out female superiority in vocabulary, articulation, length and complexity of sentences, and grammatical correctness up through the age of ten.[8] More recent studies have minimized these differences. The rationale indicates that possible environmental factors that once favored girls—such as more verbal interaction between girls and their mothers—no longer exist.[9]

Of all factors that influence the language development of the child, the most crucial one appears to be that of the family environment. The following home situations should be considered:

1. The only child, who receives all the attention from the parents,
2. The child (only or fourth) whose parents talk to him a great deal versus the child (only or fourth) whose parents talk to him only when it is necessary.
3. The child whose parents talk with him about something he saw on "Sesame Street" versus the child whose parents tell him to watch "Sesame Street" and "shut up," or the child who isn't able to watch "Sesame Street" at all.
4. The child who plays alone or with siblings only versus the child who is able to interact with many other children.
5. The child who is able to go to a park, visit a zoo, take trips with the parents, or accompany the mother to the supermarket versus the child who is left at home or taken to a sitter.
6. The child who is read to, who is told children's stories, who is given an opportunity to manipulate the pages in a book, versus the child who is never exposed to the printed page until entry into the public school.

GENERALIZATIONS ABOUT LANGUAGE DEVELOPMENT

Smith and his colleagues make certain generalizations from current studies that appear to have significance to the child's language development and to his learning processes:[10]

1. The closer the language of the child comes to the speech norms of the adult community, the more effective his communication becomes.
2. There is a continuous tendency, therefore, for the child's language to move toward adult norms.
3. The more opportunity the child has to communicate, the more skill he will develop in use of language and the more acceptable will his language be by adult standards. He needs to be spoken to, listened to, responded to.

4. Anticipation of his needs by a parent or teacher before he communicates with them will tend to retard a child's language development.
5. In literate societies, communicative need will play the same prime motivational role in the child's learning to read and write as it does in his learning to speak and listen with understanding.
6. Before change can be achieved in an individual's idiolect, the individual must feel strongly that the change will help him to communicate more effectively.

It is clear that the first four or five years of a child's life are the period of his most rapid growth in physical and mental characteristics and of his greatest susceptibility to environmental influences. Attitudes are formed, values are learned, habits are developed, and innate abilities are fostered or retarded by conditions the child encounters during these early years.

SELECTED REFERENCES

BRONFENBRENNER, URIE, and CONDRY, JOHN C. *Two Worlds of Childhood.* New York: Russell Sage Foundation, 1970.

CALDWELL, BETTYE M. "What Does Research Teach Us About Day Care: For Children Under Three." *Children Today* 1:6-11 (January-February 1972).

DEVEREAUX, E.; BRONFENBRENNER, URIE; and RODGETS, R. "Child-Rearing in England and the United States: A Cross-National Comparison." *Journal of Marriage and the Family* pp. 257-70 (May 1969).

GREENE, MARGARET. *Learning to Talk: A Parent's Guide for the First Five Years.* New York: Harper & Row, 1960.

HUNT, J. MCVICKER. "The Implications of Changing Ideas on How Children Develop Intellectually." *Children* (May-June 1964).

ILG, FRANCES L., and AMES, LOUISE BATES. *The Gesell Institute's Child Behavior.* New York: Dell, 1964.

KATZ, LILIAN G. "The Child: Consumer or Consumed?" *Childhood Education* 49:394-97 (May 1973).

SPOCK, BENJAMIN. *Dr. Spock Talks With Mothers.* Boston: Houghton Mifflin, 1961.

CHAPTER 2

Language Development in Preschool Programs

Preschool programs occur under many names: nursery school, day-care center, Head Start, kindergarten. The variety of names suggests that each program is different from all the others. This should not be true. Such institutions are not "prep" schools or trade schools for teaching some specific skill. They are schools for the development of the whole child. Each of them should help children to develop their intellectual, social, emotional, and physical powers.

Why have preschool programs? The aim of all preschool programs is to help children to learn in such a way that they spend their fourth, fifth, and sixth years in the most satisfying and constructive manner possible. Preschool is an investment in the future. According to Hymes:

> Sound programs provide experiences in literature and music and art, in the sciences and in mathematics, in the social sciences. They provide experiences in health and physical education. Children have the chance to gain in language, to expand their store of knowledge, to stretch their attention spans. Youngsters have the chance to improve in coordination, balance, speed, grace, vigor, strength. They have the chance to widen their sense of trust in adults and to deepen their sense of joy in their age-mates. They have the chance to grow in independence, in self-direction and in self-control.[1]

EXPERIENCE WITH LANGUAGE

A preschool program can nourish the speech development of children by providing them with opportunities for talking with other children. Many children will begin to talk more as soon as they start verbal interaction with others.

Children need to feel free to talk, for the verbal child has an advantage over the less verbal child. The preschool youngster, or any youngster, who is reproved for talking may decide to avoid verbal expression.

Although the curriculum of a preschool program includes such basics as concepts from science, social studies, mathematics, music, art, and physical education, it is essentially a language arts curriculum. The child is expanding and modifying his vocabulary level when he describes the action in bouncing a large rubber ball. The sensation experienced in feeling the mixture of sand and water is verbalized by a group of children as they pour water into the sand table. Feedback within the peer group strengthens established vocabulary while increasing or extending the levels of some members of the group.

Many times incidents happen that open avenues for clarification of word meanings. At snack-time Bennie asked, "Could I have one of those Africans?" The teacher viewed him in puzzlement and quickly thought back to the day when one group of children was discussing people and various races. She realized that on that day the children had dried apricots for a snack. The teacher said to him, "Oh, you mean apricots. Come with me and we'll get some!" This gave an opportunity for the teacher and Bennie to talk about the differences in meaning of the words *African* and *apricot*.

Enough cannot be said about the quality of the preschool teacher. In the example given, Bennie's teacher could have sloughed off the question or could have made a sarcastic reply such as, "Africans! How silly! Now tell me what you really want!" It is paramount that the preschool teacher diagnose the understanding level of Bennie's question and consider such factors as his listening ability as well as what activity Bennie was participating in on the day the word *African* was discussed.

THE TEACHER – A FACILITATOR

Not only is the preschool teacher an organizer of "happenings," she is a diagnostician. While the children are actively engaged in playing and working activities, the quality teacher is actively involved in interacting with the children. This is not the time to sit and observe them or to paint her nails. This is the busy time – the time for instruction. As she moves from group to group or from child to child she is listening to children's remarks, adding descriptive words here, making suggestions there, reading what is being said on their faces, trying to sense what is in their minds. She is constantly taking every opportunity that may arise out of the child's activity to strengthen and to expand his horizons — linguistic or otherwise.

She asks questions as well as answers them. The questions may be open-ended. For example, "What do you think will happen next?" she asks, pausing from her reading aloud of *Where the Wild Things Are*. Or, observing that Jim's attention span has waned from the story, she arranges for certain children to have options for various activities. When she and a group of children mix dough for baking cookies, she expands on the sound and rhythm of language.

In order to help her pupils build valid generalizations and gain sound information about good language, the teacher is ever alert to say the right words to the right child at the right time. It takes little skill to talk to children. Skill is involved in listening and in caring to listen.

Some teachers like to be on center-stage — talking and playing the role of the expert with all the materials, forever hoping that something will happen. They work extremely hard at doing all the planning, asking all the questions, answering all the questions — in the process causing children to become passive.

On the other hand, there are teachers who talk too little or participate too little. Once an activity is underway they tend to become observers. They want things to happen, yet wonder why pandemonium has set in or why aggressive children appear to be taking advantage of the more passive children. Somehow they have not found a way to develop a constructive role for themselves, to participate with children and where children are actively involved.

The wise teacher has an understanding of individual children. She knows she must be passive with one child and actively involved with another. She knows when a child will welcome words and when she should keep quiet. There are times when the teacher may be an intruder. The writer is reminded of a visit he once made to a kindergarten classroom. A small group was actively involved in organizing a puppet show and the writer stuck his head through the opening in the curtain to observe the interaction of the members of the group. The organizer of the group noticed the stranger, stopped all conversation within the group, and said, "What are you doing here? Get out of here!"

THE DEVELOPMENT OF LISTENING

Most children love to listen — it depends upon the need. In today's society the preschooler awakens to watch "Captain Kangaroo" or cartoons on television. He may hear the music from the radio of an older sibling, the buzzing of his father's electric razor, or the scratching of the brake linings of the milkman's truck. He may watch "Sesame Street" while he has his lunch. The give-and-take of the verbal interaction around the breakfast table, the last-minute instructions of mom and dad to the children before they go to school, may or may not be heard by the preschooler.

A review of some of the listening research indicates that there is a relationship between personality and listening. Kelly found that certain personality attributes, particularly emotional stability, were characteristics of a good listener.[2] Ross found good listeners to be better adjusted personally and socially than poor listeners.[3] Jackson indicated a relationship between listening and personality, and suggested that an individual's ability in using listening skills may be directly affected by his own state of adjustment.[4]

The development of listening abilities during the preschool years is important. The research listed indicates that there is a relationship between listening and personality and social development — two developmental factors that are of prime interest in any preschool program.

Although opportunities for listening may vary in a preschool program, music is an important medium. Whether the teacher herself is the musician or she plays records, music exposure can increase children's willingness to listen. Not all children may wish to listen every time such music experience is offered. Certainly there should be no compulsion about listening, for this does not build desirable attitudes about listening. Many times a child or several children will prefer to play alone on the periphery of the group that is listening to music or to a story that is being read aloud.

Some children may want to listen to records more often than others and they should feel free to do so without interfering with the play of other children or being interfered with themselves. At times a child may spend too much time listening to music — or to stories. Teacher judgment needs to recognize this situation. The child may be doing this as a form of escape from facing reality, such as attempting to adjust to other children in varying play situations. Steps should be taken to encourage the child to extend his interests, giving him more support in group relations and building self-confidence. The point is that the teacher must view the total growth pattern of the child — the social and personality growth factors as well as listening abilities.

Oftentimes children will want to listen and/or observe something that is silent. This "silent partner" may very well be the teacher.

Children frequently identify with a favorite teacher, an older brother, a father, a public figure like Johnny Rodgers or Mark Spitz. However, they seem to identify only with people they like and trust. In order to gain this respect or identification, relationships must be warm, close, and friendly. It just doesn't happen when relationships with children are cold or aloof. Children seem to have an innate ability to spot a phony immediately.

Every preschool child needs to have a crush on his teacher. He watches her every move while she is reading a story, observes her hands and fingers as she prepares the ingredients for baking cookies, is mesmerized by her voice whether she is singing with the group or speaking softly to him alone. The teacher he adores always seems to know when to say the right thing to him, when his hand needs to be held for security, and when to tousle his hair in jest.

Once the child has a crush on her the teacher is teaching every moment of the day. She is always on stand-by to listen, she is on the right frequency—always tuned-in. This "tuned-in" feeling is crucial in preschool programs, in elementary schools, in junior high schools— at all levels of education.

The beginning stage of this identification process was visible in a kindergarten classroom. While the student teacher was giving an art lesson the kindergarten teacher was seated with the children on the rug and had her left arm resting on the rug for support. One kindergarten boy, sitting next to the teacher, spent his time observing her— her face, the extended arm, the ring on her finger. His hand went out and touched the teacher's arm. On her elbow he noticed an indentation. The boy immediately examined his own elbow to see if he had the same kind of indentation.

The learnings that come through identification are unmeasurable. They may show up later—to become a part of the value system of the child—if the child thinks his teacher is a winner.

THE ROLE OF LITERATURE

Literature plays a significant role in our society. For the individual there are two aspects to be derived from exposure to literature: the expressing aspect and the receiving aspect. Marcia Brown describes the expressing and receiving aspects of literature with the following:

A picture book really exists only when a child and a book come together; when the stream that formed in the artist's mind and heart flows through the book and into the mind and heart of the child.[5]

In the lives of children, exposure to literature is a means of enriching life and developing aesthetic values as well as a form of reading readiness. One publication states:

> All the ferment in the world of children's reading grows from a conviction that books can enrich the lives of boys and girls. First of all, books bring enjoyment. . . . Books can give boys and girls the information they need to satisfy their curiosity concerning the world about them. . . . Books can expand the child's horizons in time and space. . . . Books can help boys and girls understand themselves and others. . . . Books of fantasy and invention delight children because of their own active imaginations and offer temporary release from the problems and tensions of real life. . . . Finally, through books children relive the spiritual experiences of the human race.[6]

Fortunate are the children whose parents and teacher have a love and enthusiasm for literature. Reading and storytelling are a ritual in many homes — usually at bedtime. Boys and girls ask for the same story over and over again. It is a fortunate father who hears, "Tell me the story about you and your dog and the snake when you were a little boy, Daddy!"

On the other hand, there is the forced-choice sort of reading to children as performed by an unsympathetic baby-sitter. Upon first sight of the sitter and of the book, the child might respond, "Why did you bring that book that I didn't want to be read to out of for?"

From Mother Goose rhymes the preschool child's interest soon spreads to other types of stories. It is essential that this basic interest in books be maintained and strengthened. Children recognize the magic in words and become eager to learn to read so that they can experience the pleasures to be found in books. The child who asks his teacher or parent to stop reading in order to show him a particular word in print may be in the midst of an attempt to unlock the mystery of the spoken word that has been printed on a page.

There are times when the effects of particular types of stories on children are questioned. This is a legitimate concern and should be viewed in terms of the growth and developmental patterns of children. For example, the illustrations in *Where the Wild Things Are* by Maurice

Sendak could cause concern to an adult, who might be shocked by the menacing monster with fangs and claws. About this book and others Sendak states:

> All my books are journeys, literally trips into the fantasy. It's my one theme. Through imagination kids get away from a situation — out of a house where no one is interested in them, out of a place where they're bored. Children, and the characters in my books, accept life if they know they can go away for a few minutes, have a real fantasy orgy and do all the things that are pent up, just to get it out of their systems.[7]

About violence in books Sendak states:

> When you're small, . . . book violence doesn't mean anything. You're terribly interested in anything that happens because your body and brains are still learning. Nothing is corrupt when you're small because you've yet to learn what corruption is.[8]

Because the research offers little concrete information about the effects of particular kinds of literature on individual children, the teachers and parents of preschoolers must attempt a diversified approach to literature. According to Lonsdale and Mackintosh, literature contributes to an individual's development by:

1. Providing opportunities for fun, relaxation, and recreation.
2. Helping the individual define his role in the home, school, and community.
3. Helping him to understand the interrelations of people in the society of which he is a part.
4. Acquainting him with the many ways of life throughout the world.
5. Helping him gain insight into his own personality problems and extend his understanding of the problems of others.
6. Developing pride in his cultural heritage.
7. Helping him develop his own set of values in harmony with those of his society.
8. Building his sensitivity to beauty and developing a permanent interest in literature.[9]

READING TO CHILDREN

Reading a picture story to little children requires special preparation. It is essential that certain standards of behavior during story reading be established, such as routines for signaling the "getting ready" aspects of listening to a story. Some teachers may prefer to start reading the story with only a part of the total group.

The teacher encourages a wandering child's attention by softly involving him by name or by a direct smile. Or the teacher can help certain youngsters to develop interest by selecting children to sit on either side of her as her special assistants in turning the pages of the book or in describing some of the pictures.

As a special event the child who has a birthday may select a favorite story for the teacher to read that day. It is appropriate that the preschool classroom have a table or an area where library books are displayed. Children can leaf through them at their leisure or enjoy them in a corner of the room, just as they enjoy the objects in other interest centers in the preschool classroom.

Anderson offers the following suggestions for teachers reading aloud from a picture book:

1. Gather the children closely around you either on low chairs or on the floor.
2. Sit in a low chair yourself.
3. Perform unhurriedly.
4. Handle the book so that children can see the pages at close range.
5. Know the story well enough so that you do not need to keep your eyes on the page at all times.
6. Point out all kinds of minute details in the pictures so that pupils will look for them each time they handle the book later on.
7. Encourage laughter and spontaneous remarks.
8. Make illustrations as personal as possible by relating them to the pupil's own experiences.
9. Impart your own enjoyment of the book.[10]

Within these recommendations there can be some variations. If the story is being read by a parent to the child at home there is the possibility that the parent will not be able to familiarize himself with the story prior to its reading. For a preschool group the teacher may prefer to read the story through the first time without interruption in order that the total book experience will be felt by the children. Succeeding readings of the same story would permit time for detail and for sharing personal experience with story incidents.

The preschool teacher or the parent who tries to ensure the child a pleasant experience with a picture book is providing the child with many future pleasures and insights into the world of reading. One highly desirable outcome is that of building a favorable attitude about books.

ORAL COMMUNICATION

Reactions of children to stories may differ. There is always the expected reaction, such as serious concern for the principal character and the spontaneous interaction of children who need guided time to present their views. There is the unique and quite unexpected reply—for example, this one, which was reported by a Head Start teacher. While reading the story of Little Red Riding Hood to a small group one morning, the teacher paused for a moment after completing the part where the wolf eats the grandmother. One lad appeared to be utterly dismayed by this incident in the story and with astonishment commented, "Why that dirty son-of-a-bitch!"

A speaking trend has already been established at home or in the neighborhood. Parents have contributed to the child's word power by exposing him to their own oral communication style, from which he has developed most of his concepts. Individual differences in oral language are already vast and offer a challenge to the teacher of pre-schoolers. Teachers must accept both the child who is shy and often unwilling to communicate and the child who chatters endlessly. It is a primary objective of a preschool program to help the reserved child to open up as well as to assist the talkative child to regulate his flow of conversation. Between the two types there may be no distinction in intelligence but a vast difference in kind of upbringing, in family background, in health, in sensitivity to others, and in the quality of interaction with others.

To a great extent, the child reveals his thinking processes, his attitudes, and his desires through speech. A responsibility of the pre-school teacher is to analyze the extent of the child's language growth and to take steps to offer opportunities for personal growth. Some parents have done an excellent job in advancing the child's readiness for oral communication. They have given him the names of objects and they repeat the sounds until the child has mastered them. They have taught him little songs and have read poems and stories to broaden his horizons of vocabulary and imagination.

Other parents have not been able to provide these experiences for their preschoolers. Regardless of socioeconomic background, there are children whose exposure to oral communication in the home is limited in quantity and in quality. The mother is often too busy with the other children to have lengthy conversations at mealtime. The child often goes to bed at his own selected time with little opportunity for conversation or for bedtime stories.

All preschool children, regardless of the vast differences in their backgrounds, need opportunities for expanding their oral vocabularies. For, whether we like it or not, a good oral vocabulary is a prerequisite for learning to read. If preschoolers can be provided with many activities for strengthening and broadening their oral vocabularies, it is believed, there would be fewer children with reading problems during the elementary school years.

As in the example of the boy's reaction to the story of Little Red Riding Hood, the teacher's handling of speech training and word selection at all times must be extrasensitive. When a black child says, "He aksed me for my quarter," the teacher's first impulse might be to "correct" him. But the question is: How? Should the teacher stop and teach him the correct pronunciation? Should she go into a lengthy lesson on consonants? Should she overlook his pronunciation and plan for future assistance in private? Or should she accept the child's pronunciation as a legitimate part of his speech pattern?

The current belief is that a genuine change will take place as many new concepts, new terminologies, and new experiences are assimilated. Goodman believes that schools can help children, as they experiment with new language, to handle unfamiliar concepts and situations.[11] Children, in adapting to linguistic change, go through several phases. First, there is a recognition of "alternate" forms of language. Then there is experimentation with a choice in the alternate systems of expression, and eventually an accommodation to the standard form and a gradual abandonment of the old forms.

Goodman further states:

Perhaps the only approach that may help any large number of divergent children is expansion: not the rejection of their mother tongue but expansion outward from the idiolect and subcultural dialect to the expanded language of the general culture, giving up only what is no longer needed and adding to meet new needs.[12]

The following list of speech objectives in preschool programs indicates the major expectations needed by children if they are to reveal continuous growth in oral communication.

1. To develop an adequate fund of words.
2. To provide opportunities in discussion to share ideas.
3. To increase skill in expressing ideas in sentence patterns.
4. To foster an awareness of environment.
5. To encourage favorable social attitudes in group situations.
6. To learn stock expressions of courtesy.[13]

PRESCHOOL READING

Nursery schools and kindergartens are prep schools for first grade. Right or wrong, this is the point of view of many parents, teachers, and administrators today. Perhaps the term *prep school* is inappropriate and distasteful. It denotes a certain kind of pressure — pressure on teachers to have preschool children at a certain point in reading when they enter first grade, pressure on parents to flit here and there in locating materials for home enrichment and wondering whom to believe among all the "authorities" (lay people and educators) on the teaching of reading.

This frenzy on the part of many parents and teachers has created a contagious frustration and concern about what is best for children in the long run versus hurried efforts to prepare them for a magical moment by September of a given year. It is as though we have to initiate a "crash program" in order to manufacture fifty tanks within thirty days or to train fifty recruits within six weeks. Why are we in such a hurry? What is so significantly important about being six years of age that was not of being three, four, or five years of age?

Can some kindergarteners read? Yes, a few may be reading quite early on their own initiative. Aren't American children as bright as children from other countries? If five-year-olds in Scotland are successful in learning to read, surely American children are as bright! When some American parents and teachers learn this sort of information they tend to initiate efforts to close the gap immediately.

One research report from Great Britain indicated that eight-year-old Scottish children who were taught to read at the age of five were not significantly more able in reading comprehension than a comparable group of English children whose reading instruction began at the age of six.[14]

Durkin's study reveals that many children come to school able to read.[15] An important aspect of the study, however, shows that the characteristics of early readers are good memories, concentration, curiosity, seriousness, and persistence. Most significantly, the children studied came from homes in which there was a high regard for reading and where at least one adult or older sibling took an interest in the child's reading.

This study confirms the opinion of many educators that children's oral vocabularies have been greatly enhanced by the modern environment. There is no doubt that one kindergartener of every fifty has already started to read. The question is: should the entire kindergarten program be accelerated for one child in order to change what appears to be a good program for the other forty-nine?

Should we change to a kindergarten program where groups of five-year-olds, ranging in mental age from three years and nine months to seven years plus, are grouped for formal reading instruction? While the teacher works diligently with the top ten students the remaining twenty have to do seatwork or involve themselves in a quiet activity so that they will not disturb the top group. This means that the least mature children might be doing tracing, coloring ditto sheets, or copying something of questionable value in terms of quality and time. Restlessness, boredom, and frustrations could become obvious. Moreover, reading material published by commercial companies for first-grade level might be extremely difficult for the ten bright children.

According to Sheldon, it is questionable whether even the accelerated five-year-olds receive enough advantage from reading instruction to compensate for the effort on the part of both the child and the teacher, or for the tension created in the five-year-old who might be able to handle the intellectual aspects of reading but cannot cope as well with the problem of attending to and focusing on intellectual endeavors for a long period of time.[16]

Piaget and others believe that the five-year-old needs individual attention. Children at this age profit most from learning in an informal and leisurely atmosphere, with opportunity to discuss and comment about the things they encounter in their environment. This cannot be done in a structured atmosphere where children are grouped for formal reading instruction.

Should reading be taught in kindergarten? Yes. But not as a formal subject in a structured situation. Reading instruction flows normally and naturally into the total preschool curriculum through the following activities:

1. Improvement and broadening of the child's vocabulary.
2. Strengthening of listening abilities.
3. Listening to literature.

4. Creating own stories and personal books as dictated to the teacher or aide.
5. Participation in dramatic play, puppetry, and free play.
6. Singing and participation in choral speaking.
7. Observing the manuscript handwriting of the teacher as labels and titles are prepared and displayed in the classroom.
8. Improvement of critical and creative thinking.

The most important by-product of such activities is the formulation of positive attitudes toward school, toward reading, and toward the expression of ideas. When children are free to express themselves, when they develop skills that show the relationships of the language arts, and when they see the results of their efforts, as in the production of their own books, they will feel a keen sense of accomplishment and of personal pride.

The whole issue of preschool reading is still unresolved. One major obstacle is the widespread misunderstanding of what is meant by "reading." Educators and parents should work more closely together to reach a common understanding of "early reading." If enough time and objectivity is given to the task, both educators and parents may find themselves more closely aligned on the continuum of understanding between polar extremes of disagreement.

PRESCHOOL HANDWRITING

In an integrated preschool language arts program, handwriting receives an early start. Familiarity with instruments for creating images is learned through fingerpainting, painting with a brush, using crayons and pencils. The child supplies the message—oftentimes without being asked. He is also becoming more adept in muscular coordination through these and other activities.

It is important to make use of the child's oral proficiency. Children in nursery school and kindergarten can tell stories to the teacher, who writes the words and reads them back. All children find great delight in seeing printed symbols take form on paper and hearing them again—such experience is a major step in the intellectual growth of the child.

At this point in the child's learning of handwriting, attitude is probably the most important factor. Handwriting is difficult work, and, once a piece of writing has been completed for all to see, there are many kinds of errors that can be discovered by critics. Even though preschool children are not expected to try reading their own stories, they do derive satisfaction from seeing their stories in print. This satisfaction can lead to a favorable attitude on the part of the child about the entire idea of handwriting.

At the same time the attitude of the teacher about handwriting is crucial. If the teacher reveals a personal delight in writing for the children, and in sharing her thoughts and ideas, she has performed a meritorious act—although one to be expected of her. The teacher's alertness to writing situations and her personal zeal during the writing process could be contagious for the children.

It is strongly urged that nursery school, Head Start, and kindergarten teachers establish and maintain close rapport with parents in order to provide suggested guidelines for cooperative action. Not only should the parents be provided with an understanding of the teacher's short-term and long-range objectives, but suggestions for continuing these objectives in the home are necessary. This is particularly true in handwriting readiness.

In brief, two kinds of experiences are important to writing readiness in preschool programs. The first set of experiences can be identified as those of a manipulative nature. Strengthening of the small muscles of the hands and fingers occurs through putting puzzles together, cutting, clay modeling, buttoning, and numerous other activities. Scribbling with crayon or chalk is important to the child's identification process as well as an exercise in handwriting readiness.

The other set of experiences pertains to those activities in which the child is increasing his use of the language. Stimulation of attitudes for oral expression, listening to literature, looking at and describing pictures, singing songs, creative drama and rhythmic activities, as well as dictation of stories, are all important writing readiness factors for not only the cognitive development of the child but the affective as well.

According to Burrows, learning to write effectively and for different purposes occurs most efficiently when writing is closely related to an abundance of oral language experience and satisfaction and to genuine communication with a known audience.[17] Because young children's powers of oral expression far outstrip their ability to write, their first ventures into written composition should be through dictation to someone who records their exact words immediately and visibly.

SELECTED REFERENCES

BRYAN, D. M. "Education for the Culturally Deprived: Building on Pupil Experience." *Social Education* 31:117-18 (February 1967).

CHILMAN, CATHERINE S. "Some Angles on Parent-Teacher Learning." *Childhood Education* 48:119-25 (December 1971).

CONANT, MARGARET M. "Teachers and Parents: Changing Roles and Goals." *Childhood Education* 48:114-18 (December 1971).

CONNELL, DAVID D., and PALMER, EDWARD L. "Sesame Street: A Lot of Off-Beat Education?" *National Elementary Principal* 5:14-25 (April 1971).

DEYSELING, MARY D. "Day Care: Crisis and Challenge." *Childhood Education* 48:59-67 (November 1971).

FROST, JOE L. *Early Childhood Education Rediscovered: Readings.* New York: Holt, Rinehart & Winston, 1968.

GINOTT, HAIM G. *Between Parent and Child.* New York: Macmillan, 1968.

GROTBERG, EDITH H. "What Does Research Teach Us About Child Care: For Children Over Three." *Children Today* 1:13-17 (January-February 1972).

HECHINGER, FRED M. *Pre-School Education Today.* New York: Doubleday, 1966.

HOLMAN, GERALD H. "Learning from Each Other: Pediatricians and Teachers." *Childhood Education* 48:240-43 (February 1972).

HUNTER, MADELINE. "Public Education for Four-Year-Olds: 'To Be or Not to Be.'" *Childhood Education* 49:403-7 (May 1973).

NIMMICHT, G. "Low-cost Typewriter-Approach Helps Preschoolers Type Words and Stories." *Nation's Schools* 80:35-36 (1967).

PITCHER, EVELYN G., and AMES, LOUISE B. *The Guidance Nursery School.* New York: Dell, 1964.

READ, KATHERINE H. *The Nursery School: A Human Relationships Laboratory.* Philadelphia: W. B. Saunders, 1971.

ROBISON, HELEN F., and SPODEK, BERNARD. *New Directions in the Kindergarten.* New York: Teachers College Press, 1967.

TIERNEY, JOAN D. "The Miracle on Sesame Street." *Phi Delta Kappan* 52:296-98 (January 1971).

CHAPTER 3

The Language Arts Program
in the Elementary School

The discussion up to this point has centered around the language development of the child from birth to the completion of kindergarten. The reader should take into consideration that many more children attend kindergarten than attend nursery school, day care, or a Head Start program. There seems to be a trend nowadays for increasing numbers of three- and four-year-olds to attend some kind of preschool program. For example, in an informal survey of preschool programs in a city of 100,000, the writer found that (1) most children who had some kind of nonkindergarten experience lived in the suburbs, and (2) children who lived in the inner city had Head Start as a preschool experience. The children who had no pre-kindergarten experience were mainly those who lived between the inner city and the suburbs.

The teacher of first grade or of primary one or of level one may find that the children in her group of students display a wide range of individual differences resulting from the kind of preschool program they have attended or because they have not experienced any kind of preschool program. A great variety of individual differences in rate of learning, interests, social and economic backgrounds, and numerous other factors, will be apparent in any classroom of grade-one students. These differences have a significant effect on the goals and objectives the teacher must establish for each child.

Far too many teachers begin the teaching act without diagnosing the present status of their students in understanding, use, and attitude about the language arts. Most assuredly, a teacher would want to consider the language used by the child in the classroom, as well as the language used on various tests, as data to be applied in the planning phases of the classroom operation. The effective elementary teacher will use varied and creative approaches in the gathering of data. As she greets her students at the door each morning, sits with a small group in the cafeteria, or umpires the afternoon kickball game, she strives to gain further insights into individual needs. Perhaps more practical data might be gathered in settings outside the classroom— where children are in a more relaxed environment. In order to view individual differences one may have to move into the arena where the language action is—the child's natural habitat.

ORAL EXPRESSION

Communication is important in present-day society. This may be the understatement of the era. Without oral communication it would be difficult to explain the uniqueness of a painting, the details involved in an auto collision, or the reasons why a person refused a social invitation (whether true or concocted). Throughout the school year students are called upon to give clear explanations of arithmetic problems, to show and tell, to explain social studies concepts, to discuss problems on the playground, and to participate in classroom skits. In the classroom and out there are countless opportunities for a child to experience this language arts area.

Oral expression is one of the most important of the fundamental skills taught in the elementary school. Growth in oral communication is not developed by formal instruction in a separate language class, but occurs through incidental practice in classroom activities throughout every school day. Constant assessments must be made by the teacher as she listens to the oral language of her students and gathers data for the development of future plans for action. Many elementary teachers plan an oral language program that provides sequential experiences which may be interwoven with the entire instructional program (social studies, science, mathematics, art, music, physical education, and the other language arts areas).

Assessment of individual needs must be a continuous process. Comparisons of earlier and more recent tape recordings of the speaking efforts of individual children enable teachers to analyze progress in the development of this skill. A practical approach is to make consistent use of checklists in order to compare oral communication in a particular situation with the planned objectives. The elementary teacher must assume the initiative for involving varied evaluational devices in aiding a child to develop his oral language skills.

The Teacher

Whether successful or not, whether through positive or negative reinforcement, the elementary teacher is in control of the oral language activities in her classroom. In analyzing the oral language growth of children in her classroom she may wish to evaluate the effectiveness of her own speech by recording or even making a video-tape of a lesson. The following checklist, prepared by Burns and his colleagues, should be utilized as an aid in self-assessment:[1]

1. Ability to select and organize the content or ideas of a speaking situation.
2. Ability to speak with a sincere and courteous attitude and respect for the audience.
3. Ability to speak with a suitable voice and use appropriate forms of words that express ideas clearly and accurately.
4. Ability to use appropriate posture and bodily actions.

In brief, the speaking credentials of the teacher should include the ability to express thoughts in grammatically approved sentence structure; the use of precise and vivid words; appropriate stress, pitch, and intonation; and a pleasing quality of voice. The elementary teacher with a command of the subject and a desire to communicate with children is well prepared to work for the improvement of the oral expression of her students.

Classroom Atmosphere

Possibly everyone at some point in his life has been in a class-room where he didn't dare express an idea for fear that it would be chopped off. And after it was chopped off no further ideas came forth. Perhaps everyone at some time has been in a social group where a participant captured the insight of the idea but was nipped in the bud by someone who corrected his usage. Perhaps some have been in a classroom where a child was groping for just the right way to express himself only to have the teacher or another child supply it for him. And some have wondered why a certain child was so uninhibited at age five and so turned off at sixteen.

Classroom atmosphere can be simple and free from gaudiness. The classroom is a place where people live for several hours a day, five days a week, approximately thirty-six weeks of the year. It is a place where Sam may walk over to Bill in order to discuss a mutual problem. It is a place where Beth may stand near the window and write a story that expresses her appreciation of the falling snow. It is a place where the teacher is a member of the room – not its master.

In the classrooms of the past there was an unnaturalness – an atmosphere of artificial rigidity. Eyeballs rolling in terror, students attempted to supply the correct auxiliary to a particular verb. The austere faces of Washington and Lincoln, observing from their places on adjacent walls, seemed to scrutinize the children unsympathetically. But when playing tag during recess the children quickly forgot the correct auxiliaries. And they knew that Washington and Lincoln couldn't see them throwing dirt clods in the wooded area behind the school!

Teachers who desire this rigid atmosphere in the classroom worry about the child who talks too much. The quiet, reticent child becomes their favorite – he sits quietly and completes his work without asking a lot of questions.

Types of Oral Expression

The quiet child is one of our concerns today. Our philosophy about children and speaking in the classroom has flip-flopped. Today we are interested in what Ruth Strickland implies when she refers to the idea of "freeing the child to talk."[2]

Children, upon their first entry into the school setting, come with individually unique backgrounds in speaking ability. Many of them make their entrance with speaking ability at what some grammarians classify as the illiterate level. This level may use such expressions as "he bruver," "you is," "I seed him," "he knowed it," and so forth. Such expressions are acceptable at this level, but they indicate the need for future work. The elementary teacher will reply by using the proper response but will make a mental note to work upon alternative expressions at some later point in the school year – after the child feels accepted into the mainstream of classroom activities.

The next level is touchy – the homely level. This level may use such expressions as "I reckon" and "make out your meal." It is touchy because many elementary children hear these expressions from family members such as parents, grandparents, and cousins who are worthy in their own right as human beings. The elementary teacher normally will accept these usages for the time being, making sure, however, to reply in the correct manner, but she must do so very tactfully. A mental note will be made to keep an eye on this particular usage and tentative long-range plans will commence for informal instruction.

The informal standard level is the most comfortable type of usage in the elementary classroom and is a worthy goal for attainment. It is relaxed and nonthreatening, contributing to an enjoyable classroom atmosphere. A formal standard level is more selective and may be used by intermediate students in planning a debate or making introductions when parents or guests are in the classroom.

At the top of the list is the literary level. Attainment of this level is not expected of the elementary school child.

No aspect of the language arts is more in need of constant evaluation on the part of the teacher than speaking. The child who comes to school from an illiterate home needs mammoth helpings of patience, understanding, and acceptance from the teacher and other children. He needs the best of classroom atmospheres. He must be helped, after he feels accepted, to reach attainable goals – goals that will vary from those set for other children. He must never be criticized or made to feel unworthy because of his language and home background.

The elementary teacher is responsible for helping children of all levels to establish goals that are realistic in terms of reasonability of attainment. For example, it would make little sense to place a child in a role-playing activity if his usage will become a focal point for student criticism. On the other hand, it might work out effectively to comment on his usage if student activity is centered around a study of dialect and colloquialisms.

The elementary teacher is also responsible for teaching the concept that language is a social wardrobe.[3] Through the activities in the classroom children should become sensitized to this concept. The teacher initiates and sets appropriate examples. Circumstances will determine whether it is more appropriate to say, "Shove Off!" or "Please go!" If the boys are playing football and the defensive backs are looking for the ball carrier and one says to the other, "That is he!" the tackle will probably be missed. If a second-grader is ill he would not be expected to say, "I must retch!"

The impact of positive reinforcement and humanization by the teacher cannot be overemphasized. The example set by the teacher in word and deed is extremely contagious at all grade levels. It is always open season on hypercritical teachers who express one wish but act in another way.

With understanding and a relaxed classroom atmosphere in which the child is free to speak, the elementary teacher should be able to establish a cooperative approach to an analysis of most common speaking errors and to set up a priority system for their elimination.

The starting point for any program of teaching should be the children themselves, never a textbook or a course of study. Before a teacher can improve the language of a child she must know what that language is. The notes the elementary teacher takes may show a variety of errors, some gross and some in need of mere refinement. Obviously, the deviations to work upon first are those which society penalizes most heavily.

Depending upon the socioeconomic level, the background of her children, or the geographic area, such errors may be made by only one child or by several children. The errors should be dealt with individually or with the small group that needs assistance. In view of the nature of society today, Pooley suggests that by the time the child leaves the elementary school he should have mastered the following:

1. The elimination of all baby-talk and "cute" expressions.
2. The correct uses in speech and writing of *I, me, he, him, she, her.*
3. The correct uses of *is, are, was,* and *were* with respect to number and tense.
4. Correct past tenses of common irregular verbs such as *saw, gave, took, brought, bought, stuck.*
5. Correct use of past participles of the same verbs and similar verbs after auxiliaries.
6. Elimination of the double negative: we *don't* have *no* apples, etc.
7. Elimination of analogical forms: *ain't, hisn, hern, ourn, theirselves,* etc.
8. Correct use of possessive pronouns: *my, mine, his, hers, theirs, ours.*
9. Mastery of the distinction between *its,* possessive pronoun, and *it's,* contraction of *it is.*
10. Placement of *have* or its phonetic reduction to *v* between *I* and a past participle.
11. Elimination of *them* as a demonstrative pronoun.
12. Elimination of *this here* and *that there.*
13. Mastery of use of *a* and *an* articles.
14. Correct use of personal pronouns in compound construction, as subject (Mary and *I*), as object (Mary and *me*), as object of preposition (to Mary and *me*).
15. The use of *we* before an appositional noun when subject; *us* when object.
16. Correct number agreement with the phrases *there is, there are, there was, there were.*

17. Elimination of *he don't, she don't, it don't.*
18. Elimination of *learn* for *teach, leave* for *let.*
19. Elimination of pleonastic subjects: *my brother he, my mother she, that fellow he.*
20. Proper agreement in number with antecedent pronouns *one* and *anyone, everyone, each, no one.* With *everybody* and *none,* some tolerance of number seems acceptable now.
21. The use of *who* and *whom* as reference to persons (but note: *Who* did he give it to? is tolerated in all but very formal situations; in the latter, To *whom* did he give it? is preferable).
22. Accurate use of *said* in reporting the words of a speaker in the past.
23. Correction of *lay down* to *lie down.*
24. The distinction between *good* as adjective and *well* as adverb; e.g., He spoke well.
25. Elimination of *can't hardly, all the farther* (for *as far as*), and *Where is he (she, it) at?*[4]

The elementary teacher who is serving a student population in an environment other than a middle-class community might be frustrated by the above list. In brief, her approach, as determined by observation of student behavior in the classroom, would have to be quite different. Regardless of socioeconomic factors, according to Manning, the teacher, in coping with this problem, must:

1. Develop an understanding on the part of the class of which errors are on the must list.
2. Enlist their active support in determining which of the errors occur in their own work.
3. Establish some mechanical provision for keeping a record of the results.
4. Give this record a prominent physical and psychological place in the room.
5. Organize the errors into a priority sequence for attack.[5]

Hopefully, teachers have realized from experience and from research that instruction in the development of speaking skills is often ineffective because of the following mistakes:

1. Attempting to cover too many errors.
2. Attempting to change usages that are actually acceptable forms of expression.

3. Drilling on items in the workbook whether or not those particular errors are made by the class.[6]

It is hoped that the use of workbooks will soon be forgotten, to be replaced by study of the language of children's daily living. Our language is alive and everchanging. It belongs to all — no individual owns it. Perhaps if we ever really understand this we will be able to get a few things straightened out. Until that time children should continue to view language as a colorful, imaginative, and delightful communicative tool.

Storytelling

Listening to stories has always been a part of the education of the young in the home and the community. Through stories parents have passed on to their children some of their own experiences and the wisdom they have accumulated. Mothers and grandmothers have told the children myths, folk tales, and Bible stories. Storytelling was an important part of life in many a pioneer home. Today, many public libraries provide a weekly hour for storytelling, and camp leaders and recreation directors include time for storytelling in their programs. Schools, libraries, Sunday Schools, and recreation programs have assumed responsibility for storytelling because it has come to have less prominence in many homes.

Storytelling deserves a larger place in the home and the school environment than it presently occupies. It provides warm, personal contact and a meeting of minds about a common interest, thus helping to draw adults and children closer together. Reading stories to children has value but it lacks the personal contact of storytelling.

Perhaps the reason for less emphasis on storytelling is that many teachers are afraid of storytelling because they have had no training for it. All teachers have storytelling potential. The teacher need not be highly trained or have experience in dramatics. She need only feel the mood of the story and let herself go in the telling of it so that the child can identify himself with the plot.

Storytelling is important at all age levels but it is most important to the primary-level child. A set time for storytelling, although important, is not as valuable as telling an appropriate story while children are carrying out an experience or when the experience is terminated. Stories fit into many classroom situations throughout the school day. The benefit for older children may come not only in arousing an interest, but in the qualitative improvement of their own powers of expression, and this can lead to a more sincere interest in reading. The quality of the use of language as demonstrated by recognized writers may be reflected in their own creative expression.

Dramatics

Radio, movies, and television may make children passive absorbers who are content to be forever on the receiving end of entertainment. Although television has had a tremendous impact on education, children tended to be their own entertainers prior to its advent. After seeing the latest *Hopalong Cassidy* film at the Saturday matinee, for example, it was common practice for a group of boys to reenact the stagecoach holdup in an alley on the way home from the movie. A vacant lot came alive with neighborhood boys (and girls) following the radio broadcast of the Notre Dame and Southern California football game as loyal fans played the game over and over to determine the better team. Whether there is more or less creative entertainment today is not in question here. The point is that children of all ages and at all stages need opportunities in the classroom as well as in the neighborhood to express themselves, whether as a safety valve or as a method to curb delinquency.

The school day offers countless opportunities for such expression. A social studies unit can terminate with a dramatic presentation as a part of its culminating activity. Opening activities at an intermediate level could take the form of a simulated version of television's "Today" show. Because of the rapidity and subtle message often found in a television commercial, children are naturally motivated to create their own with clever props.

Role-playing or a brief skit may enlighten a group of children concerning a mathematic concept. A simple portrayal of the Wright Brothers discussing their concerns in the bicycle shop in Dayton, Ohio, as part of a science lesson, could assist some children to further their understanding of the problems involved in early flying. This could be more beneficial than reading about the same thing in a textbook.

A collection of assorted hats could be an important purchase for a primary-level teacher. Creative dramatics calls for an impromptu atmosphere without the rehearsals that are typically required in a major play production. Long hours of rehearsal and memorization of lines could squelch all enthusiasm for future enjoyment and interest.

Drama involves people and their behavior and emotions. In today's world, we are concerned with and interested in people. In playing a role, a child steps out of himself, his own personality, and into the personality of someone else. He is freed from his inhibitions. Portraying a character may help the child to better understand himself. It may call for careful thought about timing and attention to the sequence of events. A child whose speech is awkward and inaccurate may work harder to make it more acceptable. For the child with a speech problem drama may motivate self-improvement. Drama is an integral part of living for children — as natural and spontaneous as the child himself.

Common Classroom Speech Problems

It has been estimated that about five percent of the school population have speech disorders, with higher percentages occurring in the lower socioeconomic groups.[7] Chances are that the typical speech deficiency will be an articulatory problem.

"Baby-talk" and lisping are common examples of articulatory deficiencies. Many times the child may omit a sound completely, substitute another for it, or distort the sound. While all the causative agents have not been identified, factors such as hearing loss, inadequate speech stimulation, ill health, misaligned or missing teeth, injuries, faulty learning, muscular incoordination, and emotional problems have been suggested.[8]

Since many articulatory defects clear up as children mature, speech therapy is usually delayed until the first or second grade. There are exceptions; certain problems, such as stuttering and auditory deficiencies, necessitate urgent attention. Because speech therapy is usually undertaken at the first- or second-grade level, parents and teachers must not only be the early detectors of speech problems but are responsible for correctible measures during the early years. Parents are included with the elementary teacher for the simple reason that the parents set the example during the preschool years and the child will imitate what he has heard or not heard.

Some of the normal improvement observed in children in the primary grades is due to the efforts of the teacher through speech-sound discrimination associated with routine teaching activities. Readiness activities for reading with a blending of phonics and/or linguistic skills are worthwhile contributors toward speech improvement. For certain children, this may be the first experience of having their attention focused on the sounds of their language.

Speech improvement may require considerable time. One-shot, hurry-up attempts at improvement seldom are sufficient. Time, patience, and extreme consideration for the individual are essential considerations. If there are indications of resentment, inattentiveness, behavior problems, or a refusal to speak, it may be that someone — teacher or parent — is exerting too much pressure upon the child to make a change in his speech patterns. The teacher and parent must ease up. It is better for a child to have a faulty speech sound than for him to become silent.

Perhaps at some time each of us has heard the hesitations and repetitions of the stutterer. How did the stutterer get started? It was not because he thinks faster than he talks. According to Johnson, if the child's parents become convinced that his normal nonfluencies are stuttering, they will communicate their worry to the child.[9] In turn, the child will become anxious about his speech and focus his attention upon it. Previously, the child's speech was a natural, spontaneous response. Now it becomes a thing to be watched, to be careful of, to use correctly without mistakes. Thus, the child stutters. Johnson believed that stuttering is not due to any organic or physiological disorder but is an anxiety reaction aroused by the response of parents or other adults.[10]

The following suggestions are made for the parent and teacher with regard to the stutterer:

1. Never call a child a stutterer.
2. After careful observation make referral to the speech therapist.
3. Accept the stutterer as you would any other child.
4. Reduce classroom pressures on him.
5. Support and work with the speech therapist.

Linguistics and Oral Expression

Understanding language and language usage is important to an understanding of the higher thought processes controlling the behavior of human beings. To understand the peculiarities of social patterns and the sociocentric behavior of people it is necessary that children scrutinize the many ways that people communicate.

As was mentioned in Chapter 1, a child's first experiences with language are through speech. During his preschool years, he uses speech to express himself and he gets information by listening to the speech of others. The writer remembers a mild form of confusion he experienced as a child when he was told by his mother to "Warsh your naked ears!" He understood that *warsh* meant *wash* but the *naked ears* part was totally confusing. After close examination he decided that his ears were indeed "naked" because they were often-times exposed for all to see. Many years later he discovered that the expression really meant to "wash your neck and ears."

The informal learning of English prior to attending school can be tied into the use of written as well as spoken language in the class-room. Thus, when a teacher records a child's dictation, using the language-experience approach, she fosters an understanding of the relationship between oral and written language. This philosophy is in perspective with the understanding that only a certain part of the oral language is selected to be recorded in writing.

Another form of language that must be considered by the ele-mentary teacher is nonverbal expression. This includes the use of the eyes and face and of body movements to convey meaning. Bodily movement can make a difference in the message. For example, stu-dents carefully observe the facial expressions of their teacher through-out the school day to determine how she really feels about them as individuals. The words, "Yes, you may take the basketball," spoken by the teacher with a smiling face, present a different impression than the same statement made by the teacher with an unsmiling, worried countenance.

Pantomiming may be a worthwhile activity for experimentation with nonverbal behavior. Intermediate-level students could watch professional mimes like Marcel Marceau on television, react accord-ingly, and demonstrate their own miming in the classroom. Videotapes are an excellent means for allowing elementary children to observe their own nonverbal behavior in varying situations. The teacher might gain some insight into her own nonverbal behavior from employing the same technique.

Audiotape and videotape exchanges with students in other ele-mentary schools in other parts of the United States, or in foreign coun-tries, are an excellent source for observing nonverbal behavior and for studying regional dialects. Prior to exchanging a tape the students might profit tremendously from the editing and proofreading pro-cesses employed. This activity could be much more worthwhile as a learning experience than merely reading about dialects and nonverbal behavior in a textbook and moving on to the next page.

Children who are given experience with words are able to decide which one word of several possible words best expresses the ideas they are trying to convey. Children need daily experiences with word choice, and they need to know how and why the choice of a word or expression is a very personal thing. It relates to the emotional as well as the cognitive aspect of expression. It is important that children develop an attitude of experimentation toward the language. They need to ask, "What is the best way to say this idea?" "What options are open for me?" The role of teacher and parent is to help each child expand the range of his linguistic ability and his repertoire of alternatives for use in varied social situations. The teacher or parent can help further by building a questioning attitude and a readiness not only to investigate but to respect differences in communicative techniques.

A knowledge of and respect for options in language usage may be fostered by developing an ear for commonly used patterns and also for regional and dialectal deviations. The child who has heard much good literature read to him becomes acquainted with a variety of language types and gains respect for them. Children are interested in sounds (especially in those sounds that reveal variations) and in geographical differences, and should be encouraged to view these differences as interesting but not incorrect. They are experimenters, as playground supervision may reveal, and they need to add new words to their vocabularies as well as using the old. The elementary teacher who builds a language conscience in her students will succeed in causing them to become excited about the English language.

WRITTEN EXPRESSION

Writing can play such a significant role in the overall development of a child. The four-year-old asks his mother for paper and a writing instrument. A three-year-old with a crayon stub delights in examining the markings he has made on his bedroom wall. Handwriting analysts would like us to believe that a person's handwriting can provide insights into his personality. The majority of people understand what is meant by an individual who says, "Put your John Hancock here."

The way a teacher feels about writing has a lot to do with the way she teaches children to write. Perhaps as a child she was ridiculed by a teacher, another pupil, or a member of her family about some writing she had felt proud of. Perhaps her papers were red-penciled for faulty punctuation or for improper spelling, or the paper never was placed on the bulletin board reserved for outstanding written work.

There are, no doubt, a number of children who grow up without having had a happy experience with writing. If the teacher diagnoses this attitude she can prescribe some form of treatment along with making an effort to assist such children in the development of a more positive attitude about writing.

No one would deny the importance of handwriting in today's world. Although handwriting was emphasized in the past because it was an important part of that society and time, it does not serve the same purpose today. The emphasis in teaching handwriting at the present time is placed on legibility.

Goals of Handwriting Instruction

The goals of modern handwriting instruction have deviated somewhat from the goals in the elementary schools of the early part of this century. An examination of earlier practices made by Dallman reveals the following practices:

1. An overemphasis was often placed on handwriting as a skill.
2. Undue attention was frequently paid to the mechanics of handwriting.
3. There was at times excessive emphasis on formal, isolated drill.
4. Much drill was of a mechanistic type.
5. There was little correlation, on the part of some teachers, between handwriting drill and work in the content subjects.
6. Skills acquired during the writing period often did not carry over into writing done at other times of the school day or outside of school.
7. There was in some schools a great preponderance of group instruction over individualized instruction.
8. Uniformity of style was stressed by some teachers to the neglect of individuality.[11]

To be sure, educators are still concerned with and interested in the teaching of handwriting. However, due to a number of factors (time, refinement of teaching techniques, a better understanding of principles of learning), the goals of the teaching of handwriting may be stated as:

1. To help children learn to write legibly and neatly without undue strain and at a commendable rate.
2. To allow the learner opportunities for gaining a desire to become a good writer.

Handwriting Readiness

Exposure to handwriting and the development of an awareness of it are among the prerequisites of handwriting readiness. To foster a desire to write, children are exposed to written expression. Simple announcements may be written on the board by the teacher. Dictated stories, written by the teacher, are read to the child in order to let him see the finished product. Many children who enter grade one will be able to read much of the dictated stories and will be ready for some form of handwriting instruction.

The concept of freeing the child to talk has already been discussed. This must be continued in the elementary school setting, for a child must have something to say before he can start writing. Certain activities help a child to develop the left-to-right concept. Readiness activities, which some children may have had in preschool programs (see page 26), must be continued and/or established for those children who need them. Concepts of long and short, top to bottom, and under and over can be developed through stories, games, block play, and simple comparison.

Physical activities, such as shaping clay, running, tying shoes, and using pencils, crayons, and paint brushes, contribute to the development of small and large muscles and eye-hand coordination, which are essential for learning to write.

A classroom with books available is essential. Not only must the teacher present good literature but the children should have access to interesting books for browsing purposes.

The parent and the teacher should keep in mind, during the readiness period as well as during the early writing experiences of the child, that handwriting is a skill which develops gradually through a process of continuous refinement. According to Boyd, the development of this skill is closely related to the general growth and development of the individual child.[12] Since children differ considerably in native aptitude for acquiring skill in handwriting, some will learn to write easily and quickly while others will find it a slow laborious task.

Orientation of Parents

Some parents have the impression that manuscript writing is not actually handwriting. This is quite misleading, for the term *manuscript* is synonymous with the term *printing*. To such parents *printing* implies immaturity or childishness and they often tell their children, "Now you're only printing. When you're in second grade or third grade you will be taught to write!" As long as we have the system of manuscript writing followed by a later change to cursive, teachers must do a better job of educating parents to the fact that manuscript or print is indeed handwriting.

Parents are concerned, and rightfully so, with helpful hints for use at home in assisting their children with beginning handwriting. The teacher should maintain a kind of rapport with the parents, a continuous dialogue for assisting the parent in this endeavor. The parent could receive assistance in the following:

1. An understanding of the basic philosophy underlying the readiness concept.
2. Suggestions for follow-up on use of the basic form currently being used by the child in the classroom.

Teaching Manuscript Writing

How is handwriting taught in today's elementary schools? There appear to be two distinct methods in use among grade-one teachers. The first, a structured approach, utilizes class periods of fifteen to twenty minutes in length, five times a week. According to Herrick:

> Schools favor a separate handwriting class period plus teaching handwriting in some meaningful context in all subject areas.[13]

The second approach, an informal or incidental one, is used by those teachers who believe that sufficient skill in handwriting can be gained without special practice. According to Boyd:

> The theory behind this belief is that the skill necessary for successful writing can be gained by writing and it is not necessary to single out elements for systematic practice. In this incidental or informal method, writing charts or cards with copies of the letters of the alphabet are placed in the classroom and children experiencing difficulty in letter formation are often told to refer to the chart.[14]

The elementary teacher must decide which approach best applies to her style of teaching. For the beginning teacher it is probably best to follow the structured approach until she feels competent to experiment with an informal approach.

Regardless of the approach used, before the child does much writing he should learn the correct formation of letters and the correct way to hold the pencil. These steps are prerequisites for handwriting. This should help to prevent the development of inadequate habits, which can become so firmly entrenched as to handicap the child in his early writing experiences. Then an independent use of writing skills can be promoted.

Practical Versus Personal Writing

The elementary teacher is responsible for making all children aware, early in their school careers, that there are two important points to be considered about handwriting. The first, practical handwriting, which answers practical needs, requires a quality of honesty, clearness, and expression in acceptable form. Such writing may take the form of reports, listings, captions, and plans made by a large group or an individual student. The second, personal handwriting, includes those experiences in which a child is free to express his thoughts and ideas through unique ways. Even though such writing may be trivial at the outset, children may realize that the writing experience offers a secret weapon for expressing their innermost feelings.

As the elementary school child progresses upward through the grades he should realize that:

> . . . a sense of power comes to any individual when he can fulfill the practical writing demands of his own life, whether it is the first brief direction that goes home from school or a lengthy treatise that terminates an individual study. Even more telling in its expansive effect is the personal writing through which a child expresses his thoughts and feelings spontaneously in stories and verse.[15]

Priority — Student Awareness of Social Obligation

Regardless of grade level, the elementary teacher is responsible for careful and consistent guidance of each child toward improved legibility. Children must become cognizant of the fact that handwriting must be pleasing both to oneself and to the reader. Beautiful flourishes and creative appendages will no doubt be added as individual students experiment with a unique style, but these must be channeled into the creative realm. A social awareness of the writing situation — whether personal or practical — may soon become a routine matter.

Grade-Level Expectancies

In order for the prospective elementary teacher as well as the parent to grasp the overall objectives of handwriting throughout elementary school, the following grade-level goals, as listed by Lamb, are pertinent.[16]

Kindergarten and First Grade

1. Children should exhibit familiarity (both through discussion and frequency of use) with writing as a form of communication. The teacher should utilize labels, charts, and stories dictated by children to accompany pictures.
2. Children probably will learn to write their names and usually will master the basic shapes used in manuscript writing. Many will be able to write short notes, stories, invitations, holiday greetings, etc., and most will be able to copy these from the chalkboard.
3. By the last months of first grade most children have mastered the manuscript alphabet, upper- and lower-case letters. A few will not reach this stage until second grade.
4. Most pupils can correctly write the ten basic numerals.

Second and Third Grades

1. Most children have achieved mastery of the manuscript alphabet to the extent that they can write original stories, reports, etc. By the end of the second grade handwriting has become a truly functional tool for them.
2. Children are becoming more skillful in spacing words and letters, and alignment of words and letters on a paper does not present the difficulties it once did. As a result papers are neater, more legible, and more attractive.
3. If the transition from manuscript to cursive writing is made in second or third grade, and it usually is, it is made gradually. While certain elements of joining letters, introduction of slant, etc., may be "taught" to an entire class for the purpose of saving time, it is not expected that children will make the transition with uniformity or with equal ease and ability.
4. Although children are making the transition from manuscript to cursive writing, skill in manuscript writing is maintained. Many children will continue to use the latter for independent writing activities because it is faster and easier for them.
5. Children are becoming increasingly aware of the significance of such details as punctuation, margins, paragraphs, etc.

Fourth, Fifth, and Sixth Grades

1. Children are achieving mastery of cursive writing and developing individual writing styles.

2. Manuscript writing is still maintained for labeling, map work, charts, etc. Children are encouraged to retain this skill throughout the elementary school period.

3. Children are acquiring the objectivity necessary for self-evaluation of handwriting. Teachers have encouraged this in the primary grades, of course, but more emphasis is placed upon self-help and individual responsibility for handwriting improvement in the intermediate and upper grades. Proofreading receives a great deal of emphasis.

4. A degree of mastery is achieved in fields related to handwriting, such as punctuation, paragraphing, identification and placement of topic sentences, etc.

5. Ball-point pens are used with as much ease and fluency as pencils.

The Left-handed Writer

It has been estimated that left-handed writers constitute from four to eleven percent of the total writing population.[17] Left-handedness should be viewed as just another form of individuality. It is hoped that all the furor about changing a naturally left-handed child to the use of the right hand in handwriting has been settled. The primary teacher is responsible for allowing the naturally left-handed child to remain left-handed and for providing experiences that will allow him to improve in the formation of the letters to the best of his ability.

The following suggestions should be followed when helping the child who writes with his left hand:

1. Writing experiences can begin at the chalkboard. The left-handed writer should stand away from the chalkboard and in front of his writing for manuscript; he should extend the left arm to the left so that he will be able to pull the writing toward his body in cursive.

2. The pen or pencil for both manuscript and cursive should be grasped loosely at least an inch and a half from the point.

3. If there are tables in the classroom, seat all left-handed children side-by-side and facing the chalkboard.

4. When writing at the tables the left-handed child should slant his paper to the left and make all letters exactly the same way as the right-handed child.

5. No ridicule or pressure should be placed on the left-handed writer because of the differences in his method of writing.

6. Observe the left-handed child closely in beginning writing to check for correct direction of strokes and writing across the line from left to right.

The Transition to Cursive Writing

Questions regarding the value of teaching manuscript or cursive forms of handwriting have existed since the introduction of manuscript form into this country during the early decades of this century. Most elementary teachers teach manuscript handwriting for the child's initial writing experiences. Some elementary schools teach manuscript handwriting and give no instruction in cursive handwriting at the upper elementary grade levels. Most elementary schools teach manuscript handwriting for the initial handwriting experience and follow by teaching the transition to cursive handwriting in either second or third grade.

The battle over when to make the change from manuscript to cursive continues — although the smoke is beginning to clear. Typically, throughout the nation, the transition is made each year in either second or third grade. Which is the more opportune time? Either.

Ruth Strickland is vehemently opposed to the change at second grade:

> A few schools about the country still cling to the habit of insisting that the children learn to do cursive writing in the second grade. It is just at this time that the children have reached the point where manuscript writing has become a tool which they can use with some degree of ease and confidence.[18]

At the same time the research of Enstrom reveals the following:

> . . . the learner should be introduced to the more mature, free-moving cursive script as soon as readiness arrives. To have children ready for the more advanced step, yet waiting, cannot be defended.[19]

Although Enstrom sees no real transition from manuscript to cursive, common sense dictates that if a particular child is ready at second grade it is the teacher's responsibility to initiate steps to make the transition with that child. On the other hand, if a third-grade child is frustrated with manuscript and, according to the teacher's judgment, has not mastered it satisfactorily, continued unhappiness could come to that child if he were moved on into the cursive form of writing.

Dallman makes the following suggestions for the teacher who wishes to help children reach the stage of development of readiness for cursive handwriting:

1. It is unwise to hurry the child into making the transition.
2. The best preparation for readiness to make the transition is doing manuscript writing well—with good movement, with correct position of body, paper, pencil, and in well-formed letters and correctly spaced letters and words.
3. The teacher can help develop interest in making the change-over in a variety of ways. She can emphasize that the pupils, after making the transition, will be able to write two different ways, not in only one. Although the point may be made that when the students are able to do cursive writing they will be able to write like grown-ups, care should be taken not to over-emphasize this. Otherwise the pupil may develop a disdain for manuscript writing and lose the desire to continue to do any manuscript writing after he has acquired skill in cursive writing.
4. Unless a pupil is fairly efficient in reading cursive writing, he will be likely to have considerable difficulty in learning to write it.
5. Cursive writing is decidedly different from manuscript. It should not be assumed that the latter is merely an adaptation of the former, a transition which a pupil can easily make without guidance from the teacher.[20]

The Use of the Typewriter in the Classroom

At this time very little is said about the role of the typewriter in the elementary classroom. There are, of course, some who deem the placement of typewriters in every elementary classroom to be of merit as another increment in an already overcrowded daily teaching schedule. The emphasis here would be on the teaching of typing in the elementary school since children are believed to be capable of learning to type with apparent ease.

Certain questions must be answered before the above approach is initiated. Should all children be taught to type? Only those children who are going on to college? Only those children who already know that they plan on pursuing a career as a secretary? Only those children who are having legibility problems in handwriting?

The typewriter does have a place in the elementary classroom. Many primary classrooms have typewriters with the large primary type at their disposal for purposes of typing the dictation of children. Follow-Through classrooms have used typewriters to a great advantage as a form of readiness for handwriting and/or reading. Children could benefit from experimenting with the typewriter during a choice of interest centers in any elementary classroom. As an enrichment to a learning situation typewriters do have a place in the elementary classroom. There is no urgency in the matter of a formal approach to the teaching of typing in the elementary school. Until the research is clear on the long-range effects of the teaching of typing to the elementary school student, and until the above and other questions are answered, it would seem that the place of the typewriter in the elementary classroom is that of an enrichment aid.

Creative Writing in the Elementary Classroom

What is creative writing? These days, in the elementary school, there is a kind of subtle pressure on the teacher to have the students do some form of creative writing. A teacher after reading the comments in the latest batch of creative papers, rushes to the *Instructor* or the *Grade Teacher* in the hope that some creative ideas for the children will be there.

For some, the term *creative writing* seems to imply precious writing, useless writing, flowery writing, writing that is a luxury rather than a necessity, something that is produced under the influence of drugs or leisure, a hobby.[21]

According to Smith, when an individual writes creatively, he is communicating in his very best way.[22] If writing is regarded as a communication technique, the ideas one writes are predominantly important. Misspellings and imperfections in grammar are secondary considerations.

Perhaps one should view the distinction between creative writing and other forms of writing as one of the uniqueness of the communication. Most writing communicates information—it tells the reader what the writer wants him to know. However, the creative writer goes beyond the mere passing along of information. He tickles the reader's taste buds, he amuses, he makes the reader care, he stimulates the senses of the reader. Creative writing puts some pleasure into the routine of daily operations. There is an implied feeling of relief from following the normal rules of writing, and the author instills a thread of individuality into the communication. Murray states further that:

The problem of finding something to say which is worth saying, and then saying it, is a problem which is ever new. And the teacher who shares his own struggles with his class will find that he has entered into an exciting and productive relationship with his students. He will not be a teacher, he will be a senior learner, what a teacher ought to be. And it's just possible that the teacher and the students who experience writing together may be creative.[23]

Assets of Creative Writing

Creative writing may serve many purposes for the writer. Above all, it is a means of self-expression. It is the individual's way of saying, "These are my thoughts as uniquely experienced by me." Creative writing can serve as a safety valve for dormant tensions. This implies that a period of time has evolved in which the child gave an idea some deep thought and that the message on paper is revealing of this deep, inner thought.

One of the major assets for writing in this manner is that it is pure fun. It can be a welcomed change-of-pace activity from the more formal, practical kinds of writing. It is in the domain of personal writing that the message really counts. Rule of good usage are still important but become of a secondary nature in creative writing. Creative writing may reveal certain literary talents of students who have not had the opportunity to expose their talents to others. To have a member of the peer group say, "Boy, you sure zonked them in that story!" is far more rewarding than to receive a carton of candy bars.

Finally, a worthwhile by-product of creative writing is the stimulus it gives the student to do further reading and experimentation in his area of interest. A child might become an ardent reader of good literature in order to satisfy an appetite whetted by a creative writing endeavor.

Guidelines for Creative Writing

Creative writing does not take place when the teacher says, "All right boys and girls, you have fifteen minutes until the art teacher comes. You may do some creative writing!"

There has to be a warm-up session — and each child's warm-up session varies. Therefore the teacher must extend her very best motivational powers to the occasion. The following guidelines may be helpful in this connection:

1. The classroom atmosphere must be relaxed and permissive yet have some order.
2. The manner in which the room environment is arranged can have great effect on motivation for writing.
3. Exposure to good literature can serve as a means of stimulating interest and developing writing ideas.
4. Students should not be forced to do creative writing.
5. A period of time for thinking is essential.
6. The teacher should make an attempt to reveal to the boys and girls that she too has done some thinking about creative writing ideas.
7. Patience is necessary for guiding students in the development of creative ideas.

Evaluation of Creative Writing

Evaluation of creative writing should be handled with care. All papers should receive a mental note of "fragile" on the part of the teacher. Some points to remember about evaluation of creative writing products are:

1. The teacher should not insist on reading all creative writing done by the students. If a child does not want to show his writing to the teacher, his wishes should be respected.
2. Frequently, if a story or poem is to be shown to others at the discretion of the writer, the teacher may help the pupil to correct his writing after he has made all corrections that he can without assistance.
3. Making many revisions of creative writing usually is not as profitable as spending time that might be used for such rewriting, on further writing in which the child tries to improve upon former writing.
4. The teacher should be tactful in criticisms that she makes on any creative writing.
5. There are dangers involved in criticisms by peers — sometimes more serious than those associated with criticisms by the teacher. Consequently criticism by classmates should be used with caution.
6. The teacher should guard against high praise for any piece of creative writing. If too much praise is given, the child, by contrast, may feel discouraged at times when he does not receive it. Furthermore, there is always danger that he may begin writing for recognition rather than for self-expression.[24]

SPELLING

"Children can't spell fit to eat!" comes the cry from parents, teachers, and other critics. Although children today spell better than their ancestors, we like to pride ourselves in the belief that, just possibly, we might make every individual in this nation a perfect speller. This is an unexceptionable goal—one beyond criticism. However, realistically speaking, we are working with people with many and varied attitudes and capabilities, and there is the matter of defining spelling in its social sense. The reader must reflect back to the business of personal versus practical writing in order to gain a better perspective on perfect spelling. In practical writing—yes, the spelling should be perfect. In personal writing—not necessarily, at the outset.

The teaching of the spelling of the words in the English language has always been a matter of great concern. No instructional procedures can ever alleviate the numerous frustrations that are traceable to the complexity of the spelling of our language. However, excessive concern with the hybrid nature of the English language, with the fact that it is studded with words lifted bodily or adapted from other languages, or with the lag in changes in spelling as compared to changes in pronunciation, will not solve the instructional problems.[25]

It is highly unlikely that it will ever be possible to change spelling to conform to pronunciation, and some authorities argue that this would not be desirable even if it were possible.[26]

A group of Stanford researchers suggests that children should learn:

1. To break the words in their oral vocabularies into component sounds.
2. To discover the correspondences between the phonemes and the alphabetical letters representing them.
3. To discover the influence of position, stress, and context in the choice of a particular grapheme (letter or letters) among several options.
4. To examine the morphological (meaning) elements such as compounding, affixation, and word families.
5. To use all of their sensorimotor equipment of ear-voice-eye-hand, reinforcing each through the application of the others.[27]

There has been little investigation of the results achieved by teaching children linguistic principles that may aid them in spelling.

Determination of actual procedures for helping children to discover phoneme-grapheme correspondence and to make these discoveries in an efficient manner need to be suggested.

Handwriting and Spelling

Early in the language arts program children should learn to spell the words they are currently using. The language-experience approach relies heavily on the child's use of the oral language. The leading proponent of the language-experience approach, Roach Van Allen, suggests that the concepts a child develops, as he composes, dictates, and later writes, are these:

1. What he thinks about he can talk about.
2. What he can talk about can be expressed in painting, writing, or some other form.
3. Anything he writes (or that is written for him) can be read.
4. He can read what he writes and what other people write.
5. As he represents the speech sounds he makes in written symbols, he uses the same symbols over and over again in different groupings.[28]

Children should learn the words specifically required for their individual needs as these needs arise. The total number of words taught in the spelling program is not as important as the placement of stress upon spelling in all practical writing activities and upon the supplemental spelling skills of proofreading, using the dictionary, and learning to apply spelling generalizations.

The Child's Attitude

A good speller recognizes the importance of correct spelling, endeavors to spell correctly each word that he writes, and is equipped to learn independently how to spell new words. The objective of teaching children to spell words in a basic vocabulary list is important. It is also important to develop a favorable attitude toward spelling.

Good attitudes toward spelling may be developed through continuous attention to these suggestions:

1. The teacher should regard spelling as important, as something that really matters. She should endeavor to spell correctly all words that she writes; when she has doubt as to the spelling of a word, she should use a dictionary to check herself.

2. Children should be shown that the words they are learning to spell are words that they regularly use in writing and have need to spell. Simple investigations directed at their own and their parents' and friends' writing will show this.

3. Children should be required to learn to spell only those words that spelling tests and actual writing situations have shown they are unable to spell. The studying of words that are already known is a major deterrent to the development of favorable attitudes.

4. Each child should learn to use a specific and efficient method of learning to spell a word.

5. The teacher should encourage in the class a spirit of mutual pride and cooperation in spelling achievement. Children may help one another study, proofread for spelling errors, and give encouragement to those needing it.

6. The teacher should require a high standard of neatness and accuracy in all written work. The standards should be developed cooperatively by teacher and pupils and should be consistently observed.

7. The teacher should emphasize individual and class progress in spelling improvement and make pupils aware of their progress. Records of progress may be kept by the pupils themselves and achievement should be appraised in the light of earlier efforts.

8. The teacher should immediately attack any negative attitudes toward spelling by encouraging and stimulating the children's efforts. Fault-finding should be eliminated in favor of determining the cause of spelling failure.[29]

The Instructional Program

In some school systems, it has become the practice to use spelling textbooks for each child in the spelling instructional program. Duane Manning questions this practice:

The book may actually be a hindrance in two significant ways. It mixes and confuses the basic words with those that are less basic, and it tends to introduce a rigidity into the sequence and presentation of the words that is absurd and even detrimental.[30]

A competent elementary teacher knows that a list of basic words can be interwoven with the total curriculum, and that each one can be applied, as needed, in the natural course of events. The word *valentine,* for instance, should be used in February instead of in October, or whenever the teacher senses a need for it in terms of her classroom activities. If a specific spelling principle is gained in the classroom, and if it helps a particular child to unlock the secret to a spelling generalization, then the method has proven to be effective for that child. The child who perfects an approach, or combination of approaches, is well on his way to a higher level of independence in spelling.

Spelling tests, if used properly, are basic in an instructional program. An examination of the kinds of errors made is essential. It is from such errors that the teacher and student can determine what the pupil's spelling difficulties are and how these might be resolved. A more realistic spelling test can be developed by the child and his teacher and might contain whatever words are significant to him at that particular point in his writing.

Individualized learning is a common expression with almost as many meanings as there are teachers applying it to classroom practice. *Individualization,* as related to spelling, means a completely separate program suited to each student. It is independent of a fixed word list for all children. Although spelling workbooks may be used, materials are selected on an individual basis. Thus, fast learners can move ahead without waiting for the whole class, and slower learners get the attention they need without embarrassment or the difficulty of keeping up with the group.

The basic goal in spelling is to teach children to spell the words they are most likely to need to spell in their life activities. This goal, of course, is general and must be followed with a more realistic view of the total picture. Frustration is largely eliminated through the instilling of confidence in the child. According to Greene and Petty, spelling confidence can be instilled in each child by:

1. Teaching the child to spell correctly the words he needs most in his writing activities.
2. Expanding his spelling and writing power by showing him meaningful relationships among many commonly used words.
3. Developing in him an interest in words and a desire to spell and use each word correctly.[31]

FOREIGN LANGUAGE IN THE ELEMENTARY SCHOOL

The question of teaching a foreign language in the elementary school continues to be sketchy and mildly controversial. Some proponents list two good reasons for the teaching of a foreign language: (1) because of America's present role in the world, more American children need to acquire culture, preferably through the medium of a foreign language, and (2) young children learn to speak foreign languages more easily, and with more accurate accent, than do older children or grownups.[32]

The elementary school faces a number of problems with relation to the addition of foreign languages to the already crowded curriculum. The question of time and how to fit language instruction into the daily program is uppermost. Another question is that of who will teach it? The regular classroom teacher or a specialist?

At the present time television appears to have temporarily solved the problems of cost and the shortage of qualified teachers. However, the usual problem yet prevails. All too often, schools have started enthusiastically with foreign languages but have failed to carry on the work consistently for a sustained period of years. Typically, a foreign language program will begin in a school with great fanfare, only to be found, upon another glance two years later, to have faded into a memory.

There seem to be two reasons for this pattern. First, the public, as well as educators, are not sincerely convinced that the results warrant future endeavors; moreover, there has never been a longitudinal study to measure effectively the long-range effects of such a program. A second reason is that inconsistency creates a void in the sequence of teaching. For example, French may be introduced in third or fourth grade, omitted in fifth, sixth, and seventh, and resumed in eighth or ninth grades. Until both public and educators are convinced of the utilitarian purpose of teaching a foreign language in the elementary school, the issue will continue to ebb and flow with each generation.

READING

Much emphasis has been placed on the necessity of all children learning to read. Articles have appeared in various magazines suggesting that parents begin to teach their child to read before his third birthday, or before he starts school. Doman and his colleagues say to parents:

> The best time to teach your child to read with little or no trouble is when he is about two years old. Beyond two years of age, the teaching of reading gets harder every year. If your child is five, it

will be easier than when he is six. Four is easier still, and three is even easier. If you are willing to go to a little trouble, you can begin when your baby is 18 months old or—if you are very clever —as early as 10 months.[33]

As was pointed out above (page 24), such articles are bound to stir the emotions of parents and may cause some of the more concerned to immediately go out and buy a do-it-yourself kit. Articles of a similar nature have been written by Esther Williams pertaining to teaching your child to swim at the age of four months. The problem is that not all parents have the understanding and training of Esther Williams or of the reading specialist, and thus are not qualified for the business of training their child to swim or to read at such an early age. Realistically speaking, the debate continues, with the specialists in early childhood education leading the way. The question is not so much, When *can* a child be taught to read? but When *should* a child be taught to read? A more current thought seems to be. When is *this* particular child ready to read? The time may depend on the child, the materials of instruction to be used, and the methods and procedures that follow.

Since the publication of a highly controversial book, *Why Johnny Can't Read*, in 1955, more people have given attention to the teaching of reading than at any time in history. The nation, since that time, has been caught up in the mania of why children can't read and what is the best method for the teaching of reading. For a condensed account of the advantages and disadvantages of the major approaches to the teaching of reading, see *How Children Are Taught to Read.*[34]

The importance of learning to read has become paramount in the minds of those participating in morning coffees in the neighborhood, of workers on the assembly-line, and in the minds of educators. Schools are being held responsible not only for the quality of their reading programs but for the time involved in the teaching of reading.

The Reading Process

Reading is a task that has been imposed by the culture and not one for which a child has a natural desire. The child must not only learn to read, he must be highly motivated to want to read. In order to gain a better perspective on reading, the reader should note this description of the reading process as seen by Strickland:

Reading is a complex mental process that involves the doing of several things simultaneously. The reader must recognize the symbols which represent speech and must bring meaning to what he recognizes. There is no meaning in the marks one reads – the meaning is in the mind of the reader. Little children are just in the process of learning words and meanings. To be able to decipher symbols if one could not infuse meaning into them would be completely useless. In addition, the reader must relate what he is gleaning to what he knows if there is to be any real understanding. Lastly, but actually concurrently, he must integrate what he is reading into perspective.[35]

It is believed by many that language development is the first and most important aspect of the reading process. A child must have had experience with his language in order to understand how it functions and to have a wide variety of words and meanings when he begins to read language.

Prerequisites for Reading

In addition to language development, during the preschool years the child is in the process of developing powers of visual and auditory discrimination between symbols. Parents and other interested persons can instill an interest in books and stories as well as lay the foundation for a favorable attitude and desire for learning to read.

Activities, whether reading or nonreading, which improve the ability of children to develop a span of attention and to concentrate, such as watching "Sesame Street," are also important. Learning to recognize and name the letters of the alphabet places a child at an advantage upon his arrival in kindergarten or grade one.

Freedom from physical problems, the ability to interact with other children and to focus attention on what is being taught, and emotional stability are also necessary ingredients for the reading process.

Teaching Beginning Reading – The Wheel of Fortune

As mentioned, people from all walks of life have become interested in how reading is being taught in the nation's schools. The method used during the past fifty years or so, the basal reading method, has been scrutinized thoroughly. Although the basal reading program is designed to develop readiness, vocabulary, word recognition and perception, comprehension skills, phonics skills, and a love of literature, many who regard the results believe that too many children have failed to achieve these aims. Perhaps the greatest criticism of the basal reader is that its emphasis is on reading for meaning.

Many critics believe that the emphasis should be placed on breaking the code. Supporters of this theory are centered around three methods: (1) a phonics approach, (2) the Initial Teaching Alphabet, and (3) a linguistically based approach.

Some elementary classrooms, as well as many Follow Through classrooms, are currently using the language experience approach (see page 54). There are teachers who believe that no child should be given a book to read until he has made at least one or more books of his own. This plan calls for greater organization and ingenuity on the part of the teacher.

Individualized reading, a plan in which children select the materials they wish to read from the school or classroom library, appears to be receiving greater emphasis today. Self-selection takes care of the matter of interest, and the teacher then helps the child to read the material of his choice.[36]

Information about the teaching of reading in the British primary schools has caused many teachers to peruse the research for in-depth data on how the British schools are operated. It appears that British children learn to read, but the British schools do not adhere to only one method of teaching reading. Featherstone made the following observation about the British primary schools:

> Teachers use a range of reading schemes, sight reading, phonics, and so forth, whatever seems to work with a child. Increasingly in the good infant schools, there are no textbooks and no class readers. There are just books, in profusion. Instead of spending their scanty book money on 40 sets of everything, wise schools have purchased different sets of reading series, as well as a great many single books, at all levels of difficulty. Teachers arrange their classroom libraries so they can direct students of different abilities to appropriate books, but in most classes a child can tackle anything he wants. As a check, cautious teachers ask them to go on their own through a graded reading series – which one doesn't matter.[37]

As the reading wheel of fortune continues to go around, there appear to be no conclusive results on what is the best approach to the teaching of beginning reading. According to Strickland, two major conclusions seem to stand out:

> Good teachers who are keenly interested in what they are teaching get good results regardless of method; and overall, methods

which give major emphasis to code-breaking techniques—
phonics or a linguistic approach—seem to do a little better than
methods which put their major emphasis at the beginning on
reading for meaning.[38]

There are a number of methods for the teaching of reading, none
of which are short-cuts. Each of them requires initiative, patience,
time, and good teaching. Success in the teaching of reading appears
not to be due to one single factor. The successful teacher is the teacher
who can diagnose the child's problem and come up with the solution.

As Chall noted in one of her observations about the methods used
in the teaching of reading, no one method will eliminate all reading
failures.

The best evidence that a new, even a better, method will not solve all
reading problems came from an outstanding private school that had
been experimenting with Bloomfield-type linguistic materials. Although the classes were small (approximately fifteen children per
class) and the teaching excellent (the teachers were far more qualified
than most I have met and were, in addition, aided by a teaching as-
sistant) some children were receiving remedial instruction. The new
method had been in use for at least three years, but the remedial
teacher was still performing her function, and she was as busy as ever.
My talk with her revealed that the pupils were having the same kinds
of difficulties they had had with other methods; they could not recognize the printed words easily.[39]

Independent Reading

Literature is what learning to read is all about. Reading skills are
learned so that children may read what others have written for them.
As has been pointed out, children's literature makes specific contri-
butions to the overall development of the minds and imaginations of
children. Children who read and write their own literature are usually
eager to read what others have written.

Todd, a second-grader, wrote the following story after reading
about snakes and other reptiles with a small group at the science
center in his classroom.

Once there was a plant that grew and grew till it got real big. It
turned to be a three-headed snake. The snake weighed a ton and
ran 3000 miles an hour. It had a real deadly bite. It could jump 50
feet in the air without getting killed. One day it wanted to kill
everyone in the world. Well it gots its choise it killed everyone

but the dumbest scientist in the world, he couldn't cut down a tree. But one day he tried to invent a flying pot but just then the snake came in and the scientist goofed and turned the snake into a box.

The reader will notice that not only has this student enjoyed some independent reading but he has been motivated to do some creative writing of his own. The sentence structure and spelling are as they were originally done by the student. Todd is well on his way toward the enjoyment of other literature about the world of reptiles. No doubt his interests will broaden to include science fiction and books on prehistoric life. His teacher has wisely guided him toward literature in which he has shown an interest.

The teaching of reading and the enjoyment of literature go hand in hand. In skill-building reading periods, children learn the tool skills needed to unlock the enjoyment found in the world of books. A good program in the enjoyment of literature and poetry may grow out of the first compositions of the children. These stories may be placed on the walls, to be read and enjoyed by other children. Understanding and appreciation of good literature develop smoothly when children write their own and then discover that others enjoy the power of expression through words.

Smith recommends the following as activities for building an appreciation of literature in the classroom:

1. Have a library corner with good books easily available.
2. Keep a bulletin board of good books before the class.
3. Read a poem or story to the class at least once a day.
4. Encourage children to share the good books they have read.
5. Provide time every day for children to read silently.
6. Encourage children to share their home libraries with the class.
7. Keep a time reserved for the school library.
8. Suggest good television shows.
9. Have children make their own book jackets.
10. Correlate literature with all classroom work.
11. Organize and hold a book fair.[40]

Other methods and techniques for building appreciation and good standards in literature are:

1. Dramatization.
2. Storytelling.

3. Making films.
4. Book reports.
5. Bulletin boards.
6. Displays and exhibits.
7. Contacts with authors.
8. Box theaters.
9. Shadow projects.
10. Shadow boxes.
11. Pegboard displays.
12. Peep boxes.
13. Mobiles.
14. Finger plays.
15. Roll movies.
16. Radio and television shows.
17. Murals.
18. Dance interpretations.

Comic Books and Reading

It would be interesting to determine how many children in this country, on any given Sunday morning, get the newspaper, spread it out on the floor, and (depending on the age level) commence to hack the funnies to pieces with unsure cutting hands. This operation, by its very nature, involves advantages to reading readiness. With appropriate parental (or sibling) guidance, a great number of readiness skills could be cultivated. For example, after the individual segments have been cut out, they could be regrouped according to sequence.

According to one source, comic books had a monthly circulation of over thirty-five million in 1961 and the sum of money spent on them was more than was spent on the purchase of textbooks for elementary and secondary schools.[41]

The idea of comic books is basically a good one. Due to the nature of the combination of illustrations and captions, the potential reader is able to decipher certain messages. In addition, the reader's curiosity is aroused. If viewed as a supplementary device for motivational purposes in allowing a given child to become interested in one aspect of reading, and if the control factor can be enforced, comics have a legitimate place in children's lives.

Arguments Against Comic Books

In view of the controversy over whether or not to endorse the use of comic books by children, one must admit that there is great variation between the best and the worst. Comics are supposedly written with the reader in mind, addressing the range of interests of varying age groups. Therefore it is crucial that some form of screening be involved in assisting children in the selection process. This could very well be the crux of the problem. The vocabulary level, the values portrayed, the quality of illustrations, the levels of readability, and the standards of morality are some of the factors to be questioned.

Arguments in Favor of Comics

For the preschool child, such comics as those found in television cartoons could serve to supplement an established interest in creating his own version if he is provided with the necessary paper and pencil or crayons. The upper primary or intermediate level child could be motivated to experiment with film-making in the form of cartoons – a potential creative endeavor. The nature of the vocabulary (although questionable in some comics) is somewhat more realistic in view of the way people really talk. According to the social situation, certain types of comics could be used to analyze the language of people. There is also the potential of studying the propaganda techniques used in persuasive situations in certain comics.

The Role of Comics

Obviously, both strengths and weaknesses are found in considering the role of comic books in society. It would seem that a decision to ban comic books forever is not the answer, for there are certain advantages to be derived from their use. As in any issue of this nature, the responsibility falls upon the parents and teachers to formulate standards and procedures to follow (standards to be recognized by the child) in a cooperative process for gaining the benefits that comic books may offer in the learning process.

EVALUATION IN THE LANGUAGE ARTS

As the student seeks to identify himself with the ongoing classroom activities, he is making judgments about his own current affairs. He might examine the effects of the idea-at-hand in terms of his own experiences to see if its value is what he thought it would be. The evaluative experience consists of the individual's perception of the value of the performance. According to Carl Rogers, as experiences occur in the life of the individual they are either:

1. Symbolized, perceived, and organized into some relationship to the self.
2. Ignored because there is no perceived relationship to the self-structure.
3. Denied symbolization or given a distorted symbolization because the experience is inconsistent with the structure of self.[42]

In order for evaluation to occur in the teaching-learning situation, a number of factors must be present. It goes without saying that the teacher must be a participant in this process. However, too often the evaluation stops at this point. The child should be at the apex of the evaluation procedure; after all, it is he who is being evaluated. The teaching-learning affair is a two-way operation — proceeding from the teacher to the learner and back to the teacher where the cycle continues.

Self-evaluation by the student under the guidance of an understanding teacher is essential for individualization of instruction. Judgments of the teacher are not valid until they have taken into account the evidence of the student's evaluation of his own behavior. With these two points in mind, the crucial factor becomes one of timing. At what point should the elementary teacher offer her own judgments to the total scope? How much and to what degree will the child accept or reject the judgments made by the teacher? Silberman wrote:

> Evaluation is an important and indeed intrinsic part of education. . . . essential if teachers are to judge the effectiveness of their teaching, and if students are to judge what they know and what they are having trouble learning. The purpose should be diagnostic: to indicate where teachers and students have gone wrong and how they might improve their performance. And since students will have to judge their own performance, they need experience in self-evaluation.[43]

The fostering of self-evaluation on the part of the students requires that self-evaluation be initiated by the teacher. It is essential that the teacher carry out a series of "spot checks" on her own motives, attitudes, and objectives. There must be an atmosphere of rapport in which the students become aware of the teacher's feelings and the teacher understands the depressions, anxieties, and needs of the students. The students must further understand that the teacher needs this information in order to better assist them in alleviating certain problems and misunderstandings. The mood of the classroom must be relaxed in order for learning to be maximized. To grow professionally, the elementary teacher needs (1) to know the attitude of the students about learning, and (2) the attitude of the students about her teaching ability.

Educators must not only continue to measure cognitive learning (through standardized and teacher-made tests), but must seek better procedures for measuring affective learning (beginning with observations and conferences). Consideration of these major areas must continue to be an integral part of the broad perspective of the learning process. Not only must the teacher make evaluation essential in her classroom routine with students, but she must gain the cooperation of the parents in the evaluational process.

The burden of responsibility rests on the shoulders of the individual elementary teacher. It is through her initiative and creative abilities that experimentation in the development of techniques and procedures for evaluating individual growth in student attitudes, values, habits, and personal interests will transpire. In order to assist the individual teacher in this responsibility, a sensitivity for the total welfare of all students must be present and, if not present, attempts must be made to develop it even if there are adverse and negative social conditions. Teachers must continue to grow professionally through their teaching experiences. As Arthur Combs has said:

> The challenge to education is not to remove all limits, but to provide a stable structure which enables children to define the situation, to understand relationships and to evaluate their own behavior.[44]

Evaluating Progress

Evaluation, as defined in this context, is the process of determining the extent to which objectives have been achieved. It includes all procedures used by the teacher, students, and school personnel to appraise the outcomes of instruction. More specifically evaluation involves such steps as:

1. Formulating goals as behaviors.
2. Gathering evidence on the achievement of goals in selected situations.
3. Summarizing and recording evidence.
4. Interpreting evidence.
5. Using interpretations to improve instruction.

Evaluational techniques include:

1. Teacher-made tests.
2. Standardized tests.
3. Questionnaires.
4. Observations.
5. Checklists.
6. Inventories.
7. Diaries, logs, and other forms of written work.
8. Diagnostic tests.
9. Rating scales.
10. Any other instrument with which teachers can gain evidence of a change in student behavior.

Evaluation should include teacher evaluation, teacher-pupil evaluation, pupil self-evaluation, and pupil-pupil evaluation.

The following is an example of some of the skills and evaluative techniques that an elementary teacher could implement for gathering data on the progress of individual students:

EVALUATION OF INDIVIDUAL PROGRESS

SKILLS	EVALUATIVE TECHNIQUE
Ability to acquire needed vocabulary	Listen for content in child's talk, for speech problems, for voice qualities.
	Can child describe or indicate different meanings?
	Does the child use them in his own speech?
Usage	Can child identify idioms of speech?
	Does the child recognize slang and is it a part of his speech?
	Is the child revealing an interest in word origins?
Creative expression	Are students using new and colorful language in their speaking?
	Can students use precise terms in giving descriptions?
	Are more ideas created in a group situation or on an individual basis?
	Can the student make up situations that may be dramatized?

SKILLS	EVALUATIVE TECHNIQUE
Conversation	Does the child share ideas?
	Does the child stick to the topic and add to an idea already expressed?
	Does the child relate tactfully and is he revealing an awareness that language is a social wardrobe?
	Is the child considerate of differences of opinion?
Voice improvement	Is there improvement in enunciation and tonal quality?
	Can the child show different moods with his voice?
	Can the child show varied meanings of the same words?
	Does the child say the letter consistently in correct form?
Listening	Can the child hear his own correct and incorrect pronunciation?
	Does the child hear the difference in speech sounds? Letter sounds?
	Does speech improve with choral work?
	Can the child distinguish sounds that are alike and almost alike?
	Does the child listen well in all situations?
Sentence structure	Do students use longer and more interesting sentence forms in speech and writing?
Handwriting readiness	Does the child appear to be interested and does he participate in dictation?
	Is the child able to discriminate and make letters?
	Does the child use one hand more frequently than the other?
Manuscript	Is the child able to follow instructions?
	Are there spaces between letters and between words?
	Are devices helpful?
	Can the child recognize his errors?
	Are slant and strokes improving?

SKILLS	EVALUATIVE TECHNIQUE
Left-handed writer	Is there proper placement of paper and direction of strokes?
Cursive	Can the child observe the steps in adding cursive?
	Can the child maintain good manuscript while transferring to cursive?
	Is there improvement in general appearance of cursive handwriting?
	Does legibility change under varying degrees of speed?
Spelling	Is the child able to find and correct his mistakes?
	Does the child demonstrate the use of generalizations?
	Is the child finding his own individual scheme for spelling improvement?
	Has the child's attitude about spelling improved?
Mechanics	Does the child use appropriate punctuation marks in written work?
	Does the child show use of punctuation marks with his voice?
References	Does the child use reference materials in his writing?
Imaginative writing	Does creative imagination produce unique ideas?
	Do the stories reveal a deep inner feeling?
Dramatizations	Is the child able to demonstrate varied feelings and reactions to indicate an understanding of the various ways in which people react in different situations?
	Is the child gaining skill in self-expression, social participation, and self-confidence?
	What attitudes has the child developed pertaining to differences of others?

SELECTED REFERENCES

ALLEN, EVELYN YOUNG. "What the Classroom Teacher Can Do for the Child with Speech Defects." *NEA Journal* 56:35-36 (November 1967).

ALLEN, JOAN GORE. "Creative Dramatics and Language Arts Skills." *Elementary English* 46:436-37 (April 1969).

ANDERSON, PAUL S., ed. *Linguistics in the Elementary School Classroom.* New York: Macmillan, 1971.

BACHRACH, BEATRICE. "Dirty Words in the Classroom." *Elementary English* 48:998-99 (December 1971).

BENDER, KENNETH R. "Using Brighter Students in a Tutorial Approach to Individualization." *Peabody Journal of Education* 45:156-57 (November 1967).

BIBERSTINE, RICHARD D. "Fourth Graders Do Write About Their Problems." *Elementary English* 45:731-35 (October 1968).

BLACKMAN, MILDRED R. "Conversation, A Skill to be Learned." *Elementary English* 48:797-99 (November 1971).

BLAKE, HOWARD E. "Written Composition in English Primary Schools." *Elementary English* 48:605-16 (October 1971).

BORDIE, JOHN G. "When Should Instruction in a Second Language or Dialect Begin?" *Elementary English* 48:551-58 (May 1971).

BOYD, GERTRUDE A., and TALBERT, E. GENE. *Spelling in the Elementary School.* Columbus: Charles E. Merrill, 1971.

BROTHERS, AILEEN, and HOLSCLAW, CORA. "Fusing Behaviors into Spelling." *Elementary English* 46:25-28 (January 1969).

BURROWS, ALVINA TRUET. "Children's Language: New Insights for the Language Arts." *National Elementary Principal* 55:16-21 (September 1965).

BUTTS, DAVID P. "Content and Teachers in Oral Language Acquisition — Means or Ends?" *Elementary English* 48:290-97 (March 1971).

CHALL, JEANNE. *Learning to Read: The Great Debate.* New York: McGraw-Hill, 1967.

CHANDLER, THEODORE A. "Reading Disability and Socio-Economic Status." *Journal of Reading* 10:5-21 (October 1966).

COLLINS, NORA. "I Ain't Got None." *Elementary English* 44:35-36 (January 1967).

CONDON, ELAINE C. "Foreign Languages in the Elementary School." In *Elementary Education: Current Issues and Research in Education,* edited by MAURIE HILLSON. New York: Free Press, 1967.

DALE, EDGAR. "Vocabulary Development of the Underprivileged Child." *Elementary English* 42:778-86 (November 1965).

DAVIS, ALLISON. "Teaching Language and Reading to Disadvantaged Negro Children." *Elementary English* 42:791-97 (November 1965).

DOWNING, JOHN. "What's Wrong with I.T.A.?" *Phi Delta Kappan* 48:262-65 (February 1967).

DUKER, SAM. *Teaching Listening in the Elementary School.* Metuchen, N.J.: Scarecrow Press, 1971.

ENDRES, RAYMOND J. "Children and Poetry." *Elementary English* 40:838-42 (December 1963).

ENSTROM, E. A., and ENSTROM, DORIS C. "Signs of Readiness." *Elementary English* 48:215-20 (February 1971).

FENNIMORE, FLORA. "Creative Ways to Extend Children's Literature." *Elementary English* 48:209-14 (April 1971).

FURNER, BEATRICE A. "The Perceptual-Motor Nature of Learning in Handwriting." *Elementary English* 46:886-94 (November 1969).

GETZELS, J. W., and JACKSON, P. W. *Creativity and Intelligence: Explorations with Gifted Students.* New York: John Wiley, 1962.

GIBBS, VANITA. "Syntactic Sources for Studying Structure." *Contemporary Education* 40:230-32 (February 1969).

GILSON, JACK, and PAST, RAY. "Listening and Response Theory: Implications for Linguistically Different Learners." *Elementary English* 47:1060-66 (December 1970).

GOLUB, LESTER S. "Stimulating and Perceiving Children's Writing: Implications for an Elementary Writing Curriculum." *Elementary English* 48:33-49 (January 1971).

HANNA, PAUL R.; HODGES, RICHARD E.; and HANNA, JEAN S. *Spelling: Structure and Strategies.* Boston: Houghton Mifflin, 1971.

HARRIS, LARRY A. "Evaluating a Reading Program at the Elementary Grade Level." In *Measurement and Evaluation of Reading,* edited by ROGER FARR. New York. Harcourt, Brace & World, 1970.

HEATHCOTE, DOROTHY. "How Does Drama Serve Thinking, Talking, and Writing?" *Elementary English* 47:1077-81 (December 1970).

HERMAN, WAYNE L. "Is the Display of Creative Writing Wrong?" *Elementary English* 47:35-38 (January 1970).

HERRICK, VIRGIL E. "Manuscript and Cursive Writing." *Childhood Education* 37:264-67 (February 1961).

HILDRETH, GERTRUDE. "Manuscript Writing After Sixty Years." *Elementary English* 37:3-13 (January 1960).

_____. "Simplified Handwriting for Today." *Journal of Educational Research* 56:330-33 (February 1963).

HILLERICH, ROBERT L. "Evaluation of Written Language." *Elementary English* 48:839-42 (November 1971).

HUSSAIN, DONNA. "Is the Teaching of Foreign Languages in the Elementary School Worthwhile?" *Elementary English* 40:821-24 (December 1963).

JACOBS, LELAND B. "Humanisms in Teaching Reading." *Phi Delta Kappan* 52:464-67 (April 1971).

JENKINS, ESTHER C. "Multi-Ethnic Literature: Promise and Problems." *Elementary English* 50:694-700 (May 1973).

JOHNSON, KENNETH R. "Teachers' Attitude Toward the Nonstandard Negro Dialect." *Elementary English* 48:176-84 (February 1971).

KEENER, BEVERLY M. "Individualized Reading and the Disadvantaged." *Reading Teacher* 20:410-12 (February 1967).

KUSE, HILDEGARD, R., and ALLAR, BETTY. "I Write More Better with a Partner." *Elementary English* 48:984-88 (December 1971).

KYTE, GEORGE C. "Supervisory Visits to Classrooms Disclose Teachers' Incorrect Speech Habits." *Educational Forum* 25:489-97 (May 1961).

LAMB, POSE. *Linguistics in Proper Perspective.* Columbus: Charles E. Merrill, 1967.

LANDRY, DONALD L. "The Neglect of Listening." *Elementary English* 46:599-605 (May 1969).

LANGER, JOHN H. "Non-Standard Spelling and Language Experience in Beginning Reading." *Elementary English* 48:951-52 (December 1971).

LARSON, KAREN, and SWAN, JEANNE. "Spelling the Words They Need Today — An Individualized Approach." *NEA Journal* 55:51-52 (February 1966).

LARSON, RICHARD L. "Rhetorical Writing in Elementary School." *Elementary English* 48:926-31 (December 1971).

LENNON, ROGER T. "What Can Be Measured?" *Reading Teacher* 15:326-37 (March 1962).

MCDONALD, ARTHUR S. "Some Pitfalls in Evaluating Progress in Reading Instruction." *Phi Delta Kappan* 46:336-38 (April 1964).

MCFETRIDGE, PATRICIA L. "Evaluation and the Task." *Elementary English* 48:203-208 (February 1971).

MACKINTOSH, HELEN K. "Catching Color and Rhythm in Poetry with Nine-Year-Olds." *Elementary English* 48:81-85 (January 1971).

MILLER, ETHEL BERYL. "Listen-to Hear." *Elementary English* 45:1071-72 (December 1968).

MILLER, JACK W., and MILLER, HAROLDINE G. "Individualizing Instruction Through Diagnosis and Evaluation." *Childhood Education* 46:417-21 (May 1970).

MILLER, NARNIE E. "What Creative Writing Can Tell a Teacher About Children." *Elementary English* 44:273-74 (March 1967).

OKSENDAHL, WILMA J. "Keyboard Literacy for Hawaii's Primary Children." *Educational Horizons* 51:20-27 (Fall 1972).

PERRODIN, ALEX F., and SNIPES, WALTER T. "The Relationship of Mobility to Achievement in Reading, Arithmetic, and Language in Selected Georgia Elementary Schools." *Journal of Educational Research* 59:315-19 (March 1966).

PERSONKE, CARL, and YEE, ALBERT H. "The Situational Choice and the Spelling Program." *Elementary English* 45:32-37 (January 1968).

PLATTOR, EMMA E., and WOESTEHOFF, ELLSWORTH S. "Toward a Singular Style of Instruction in Handwriting." *Elementary English* 48:1009-11 (December 1971).

PONDER, EDDIE G. "Understanding the Language of the Culturally Disadvantaged Child." *Elementary English* 42:769-74 (November 1965).

REDDIN, ESTOY. "Writing in Another Language." *Elementary English* 48:643-47 (October 1971).

REUTER, ALEX. "Listening Experiences: Instructional Materials Center Dial-A-Tape System Advances Learning." *Elementary English* 46:905-6 (November 1969).

SCOTT, ROBERT IAN. "Teaching Elementary English Grammar with Color-Coded Word Blocks." *Elementary English* 45:972-81 (November 1968).

SCOTT, WESLEY E. "The Lost Art of Handwriting." *Science Digest* 48:364-66 (December 1960).

SHAPIRO, PHYLLIS P., and SHAPIRO, BERNARD J. "Two Methods of Teaching Poetry Writing in the Fourth Grade." *Elementary English* 48:225-28 (April 1971).

SHAY, D'ARCY C. "Creativity in the Classroom." *Elementary English* 48:1000-1 (December 1971).

SMITH, HOLLY. "Standard or Nonstandard: Is There an Answer?" *Elementary English* 50:225-35 (February 1973).

STAUFFER, R. G. *Teaching Reading as a Thinking Process.* New York: Harper & Row, 1969.

STRICKLAND, RUTH G. "The Teaching of Grammar." *National Elementary Principal* 55:59-62 (November 1965).

_____. "The Real Issues in the Great Language Controversy." *English Journal* 55:28-33 (January 1966).

TIBBITS, A. M. "The Grammatical Revolution That Failed." *Elementary English* 45:44-50 (January 1968).

TIEDT, SIDNEY W. "Self Involvement in Writing." *Elementary English* 44:475-79 (May 1967).

TOWNEY, SHIRLEY. "An Analysis of the Ball Point Pen Versus the Pencil as a Beginning Handwriting Instrument." *Elementary English* 44:59-61 (January 1967).

VALMONT, WILLIAM J. "Spelling Consciousness: A Long Neglected Area." *Elementary English* 49:1219-22 (December 1972).

VOLC, JUDY, and STUART, ALLAIRE. "Storytelling in the Language Arts Program." *Elementary English* 45:958-65 (November 1968).

WILT, MIRIAM E. "Organizing for Language Learning." *National Elementary Principal* 55:6-12 (November 1965).

WYNN, SAMMYE J. "A Beginning Reading Program for the Deprived Child." *Reading Teacher* 21:40-47 (October 1967).

Notes

CHAPTER 1

1. Ruth Weir, *Language in the Crib* (The Hague: Mouton, 1962).

2. Noam Chomsky, review of *Verbal Behavior* by B. F. Skinner, *Language* 35:26-58 (1959).

3. Susan M. Ervin and Wick R. Miller, "Language Development," *Child Psychology*, NSSE Yearbook 62, 1:135 (1963).

4. Herbert Ginsburg and Sylvia Opper, *Piaget's Theory of Intellectual Development* (Englewood Cliffs, N.J.: Prentice Hall, 1969), p. 85.

5. Joe Frost, *Guiding Children's Language Learning*, ed. Pose Lamb (Dubuque: William C. Brown, 1967), p. 19.

6. John Einsenson and Mardel Ogilvie, *Speech Correction in the Schools*, 2d ed. (New York: Macmillan, 1963), p. 104.

7. Arthur Jensen, "How Much Can We Boost IQ and Scholastic Achievement?" *Harvard Educational Review* 39:1-123 (Winter 1969).

8. Dorothy McCarthy, *The Language Development of the Preschool Child*, Institute of Child Welfare Monograph Series no. 4 (Minneapolis: University of Minnesota Press, 1930).

9. Harris Winitz, "Language Skills of Male and Female Kindergarten Children," *Journal of Speech and Hearing Disorders* 2:377-85 (December 1959).

10. Brooks Smith, Kenneth Goodman, and Robert Meredith, *Language and Thinking in the Elementary School* (New York: Holt, Rinehart & Winston, 1970), p. 12.

CHAPTER 2

1. James L. Hymes, Jr., *Teaching the Child Under Six* (Columbus: Charles E. Merrill, 1968), p. 3.

2. Charles Kelly, "Mental Ability and Personality Factors in Listening," *Quarterly Journal of Speech* 49:152-56 (April 1963).

3. Ramon Ross, "A Look at Listeners," *Elementary School Journal* 64:369-72 (April 1964).

4. Ann Elizabeth Jackson, "An Investigation of the Relationship Between Listening and Selected Variables in Grades 4, 5, and 6," *Dissertation Abstracts* 27:53A (July 1966).

5. Marcia Brown, "Acceptance Paper. Caldecott Medal Books 1938-1957" (Boston: Horn Book).

6. National Council of Teachers of English, Commission on the English Curriculum, *Language Arts for Today's Children*, NCTE Curriculum Series (New York: Appleton-Century-Crofts, 1954), vol. 2.

7. Dallas Galvin, "Maurice Sendak Observes Children's Literature," *Harper's Bazaar* 3133:103 (December 1972).

8. Ibid.

9. Bernard J. Lonsdale and Helen K. Mackintosh, *Children Experience Literature* (New York: Random House, 1973), p. 24.

10. Paul S. Anderson, *Language Skills in Elementary Education*, 2d ed. (New York: Macmillan, 1972), p. 151.

11. Kenneth S. Goodman, "Let's Dump the Uptight Model in English," *Elementary School Journal* 69:1-13 (October 1969).

12. Kenneth S. Goodman et al., *Language and Thinking in the Elementary School* (New York: Holt, Rinehart & Winston, 1970), p. 56.

13. Helen Hefferman, *Guiding Children's Language Learning*, ed. Pose Lamb, 2d ed. (Dubuque: William C. Brown, 1967), p. 150.

14. P. E. Vernon, M. B. O'Gorman, and T. McClellan, "Comparative Study of Educational Attainments in England and Scotland," *British Journal of Educational Psychology* 25:195-203 (1955).

15. Dolores Durkin, "Children Who Read Before Grade One," *Reading Teacher* 14:163-66 (January 1961).

16. William D. Sheldon, "Research Related to Teaching Kindergarten Children to Read," in *Reading in the Kindergarten?* (Washington: Association for Childhood Education International, 1963), pp. 16-17.

17. Alvina Burrows et al., *New Horizons in the Language Arts* (New York: Harper & Row, 1972), p. 242.

CHAPTER 3

1. Paul C. Burns et al., *The Language Arts in Childhood Education*, 2d ed. (Chicago: Rand McNally, 1971), p. 143.

2. Ruth Strickland, *The Language Arts in the Elementary School*, 3d ed. (Lexington, Mass.: D. C. Heath, 1969), p. 144.

3. Ibid., p. 158.

4. Robert C. Pooley, "Dare Schools Set a Standard in English Usage?" *English Journal* 49:179-80 (March 1960).

5. Duane Manning, *The Qualitative Elementary School* (New York: Harper & Row, 1963), p. 46.

6. Mildred A. Dawson, "A Summary of Research Concerning English Usage," *Elementary English* 28:141-47 (March 1951).

7. Gerald M. Phillips et al., *The Development of Oral Communication in the Classroom* (New York: Bobbs-Merrill, 1970), p. 118.

8. Ibid.

9. Wendell Johnson et al., *Speech Handicapped School Children* (New York: Harper & Row, 1967).

10. Ibid.

11. Martha Dallman, *Teaching the Language Arts in the Elementary School*, 2d ed. (Dubuque: William C. Brown, 1971), p. 158.

12. Gertrude A. Boyd, *Teaching Communication Skills in the Elementary School* (New York: Van Nostrand Reinhold, 1970), p. 41.

13. Virgil Herrick, *New Horizons for Research in Handwriting* (Madison: University of Wisconsin Press, 1963), p. 20.

14. Boyd, *Teaching Communication Skills*, p. 41.

15. Alvina T. Burrows, Doris C. Jackson, and Dorothy O. Sanders, *They All Want to Write: Written English in the Elementary School*, 3d ed. (New York: Holt, Rinehart & Winston, 1964), p. 2.

16. Pose Lamb, *Guiding Children's Language Learning* (Dubuque: William C. Brown, 1971), pp. 212-14.

17. Paul S. Anderson, *Language Skills in Elementary Education*, 2d ed. (New York: Macmillan, 1972), p. 203.

18. Strickland, *Language Arts*, p. 310.

19. E. A. Enstrom, "But How Soon Can We Really Write?" *Elementary English* 45:360-63 (March 1968).

20. Dallman, *Teaching the Language Arts*, p. 173.

21. Donald M. Murray, "Why Creative Writing Isn't—Or Is," *Elementary English* 50:523-25 (April 1973).

22. James A. Smith, *Adventures in Communication: Language Arts Methods* (Boston: Allyn & Bacon, 1972), p. 326.

23. Donald M. Murray, "Stimulating Creativity," *Elementary English* 50:521 (April 1973).

24. Dallman, *Teaching the Language Arts*, pp. 295-96.

25. Jean S. Hanna and Paul R. Hanna, "Spelling as a School Subject: A Brief History," *National Elementary Principal* 38:9 (May 1959).

26. William J. Stevens, "Obstacles to Spelling Reform," *English Journal* 54:85-90 (February 1965).

27. Paul R. Hanna and Jean S. Hanna, "Applications of Linguistics and Psychological Cues to the Spelling Course of Study," *Elementary English* 42:735-59 (November 1965).

28. Roach Van Allen, "The Write Way to Read," *Elementary English* 44:480-85 (May 1967).

29. Harry A. Greene and Walter T. Petty, *Developing Language Skills in the Elementary Schools* (Boston: Allyn & Bacon, 1967), p. 326.

30. Manning, *Qualitative Elementary School*, p. 55.

31. Greene and Petty, *Developing Language Skills*, pp. 322-23.

32. Afton D. Nance, "Teaching English to Speakers of Other Languages," in *On Teaching English to Speakers of Other Languages*, ed. Carol J. Kreider (Champaign, Ill.: National Council of Teachers of English, 1966).

33. Glenn Doman, George L. Stevens, and Reginald C. Orem, "You Can Teach Your Baby to Read," *Ladies' Home Journal* 80:62 (May 1963).

34. Carole Matthes, *How Children Are Taught to Read* (Lincoln: Professional Educators Publications, 1972).

35. Strickland, *Language Arts*, p. 256.

36. Jeannette Veatch, *Reading in the Elementary School* (New York: Ronald Press, 1966).

37. Joseph Featherstone, "The Primary School Revolution in Britain," *New Republic* (August 10, 1967).

38. Strickland, *Language Arts*, p. 274.

39. Jeanne Chall, "What Rationales Can You Come to About Reading?" *Instructor* 77:93-94 (March 1968).

40. Smith, *Adventures in Communication*, p. 293.

41. Anna Wolf, "TV, Movie, Comics, Boon or Bane to Children?" *Parents' Magazine* 36:47 (April 1961).

42. Carl R. Rogers, *Client Centered Therapy* (Boston: Houghton Mifflin, 1951), p. 503.

43. Charles E. Silberman, *Crisis in the Classroom: The Remaking of American Education* (New York: Random House, 1970), p. 138.

44. Arthur Combs, *Perceiving, Behaving, Becoming: A New Focus for Education*, ASCD Yearbook (Washington: Association for Supervision and Curriculum Development, 1962), p. 238.

Index

Art, 19

Baby-sitter, 19

"Captain Kangaroo," 16

Classroom atmosphere, 31

Day care, 14, 29

Drama, 27, 37

Evaluation, 64

Foreign language, 56

Handwriting
  attitude, 26
  creative, 50, 62
  cursive, 48
  dictation, 26, 27
  left-handedness, 47
  manuscript, 43, 44
  readiness, 12, 26, 27, 41, 42, 49

Head Start, 14, 22, 27, 29

Intelligence, 11

Kindergarten, 14, 16, 24, 25, 27, 29

Language-experience approach, 26, 49, 54, 60

Language experimentation, 10, 11, 14

Linguistics, 9, 10, 23, 39, 40, 53

Listening, 16, 17, 18

Literature, 12, 16, 18, 19, 20, 21, 62

Mother Goose, 19

Music, 17

Nursery school, 14, 27, 29

Pantomiming, 40

Parents, 8, 9, 11, 12, 17, 22, 23, 24, 27, 38, 39, 40, 43

Personality, 16

Picture books, 20-21

Reading
  comic books, 63-64
  independent, 61, 62
  methods, 59-61
  preschool, 57-58
  process, 58
  readiness, 19, 20-21, 24, 26-27, 58, 59

Role playing, 37

"Sesame Street," 12, 17

Speaking, 22
  levels of, 32, 33

Speech development, 14-15, 26

Speech models, 10, 31, 37

Speech organs, 11

Speech problems
  articulation, 38
  baby talk, 38
  stuttering, 39

Spelling, 53-54
  attitude, 54
  handwriting, 54
  individualized, 55

Storytelling, 19, 36

Teacher, elementary, 31, 33-34, 38-39, 40, 43, 55, 66

Teacher, preschool, 15, 16, 17, 18, 22, 23, 24

Typewriter, 49

Usage, 33-34, 35

Verbal gratification, 9

Vocabulary development, 8, 9, 10, 14, 15, 16, 24-25, 27, 30, 32-33, 38-39, 40-41

sex differences, 11-12

Vocalization, 8-9